Between Method and Madness—Essays on Swedenborg and Literature marks the fourth volume of the Journal of the Swedenborg Society and the second on Swedenborg's relation to Literature. For information on previous volumes please contact: The Swedenborg Society, 20-21 Bloomsbury Way, London WC1A 2TH, England.

Between Method and Madness—
Essays on Swedenborg
and Literature

Between Method and Madness—
Essays on Swedenborg
and Literature

Edited and introduced by

Stephen McNeilly

Journal of the Swedenborg Society
Swedenborg House
20-21 Bloomsbury Way
London WC1A 2TH

—

2005

ACKNOWLEDGEMENTS
Special thanks to Caroline Curtis, Richard Lines, Paul McNeilly,
Louise Martin and Lara Lynn Muth for their suggestions, comments and assistance.

Adelheid Kegler's article 'Elements of Swedenborgian Thought in Symbolistic Landscapes:
with reference to Sheridan Le Fanu and George MacDonald' was translated from the German
by Alan Stott. Endnotes to 'Swedenborg, Mediums and the Desolate Places' and
'The Story of Swedenborg' compiled by James Wilson.

Volume four of the 'Journal of the Swedenborg Society'.

Enquiries concerning guidelines
for submission, editorial policy and information on future editions
should be directed to the Editor at the address below.

Editor: Stephen McNeilly
Assistant Editors: Victoria Gordon and James Wilson

Published by:
The Swedenborg Society
Swedenborg House
20-21 Bloomsbury Way
London WC1A 2TH

Book design and artwork: Stephen McNeilly
Cover photograph: Kathleen McNeilly © 2005 Stephen McNeilly

Typeset at Swedenborg House
Printed and bound in Great Britain at the University Press,
Cambridge

ISBN 0 85448 145 1
British Library Cataloguing-in-Publication Data
A catalogue record for this book is available
from the British Library

Table of Contents

———

Table of Contents

Contributors

Arthur Conan Doyle (1859-1930), the creator of two of modern literature's best known and most loved characters in the form of detective Sherlock Holmes and his assistant Dr Watson. Holmes made his debut in *A Study in Scarlet* (1887) and went on to feature in the novels *The Sign of Four* (1889), *The Hound of the Baskervilles* (1902) and *The Valley of Fear* (1915). Doyle was also the author of *The Land of Mist* (1926), *The Lost World* (1912), *The Exploits of Brigadier Gerard* (1896), *The Adventures of Gerard* (1903), *Micah Clarke* (1889), *The White Company* (1891), *The Great Boer War* (1900) and two books on Spiritualism entitled *The History of Spiritualism* (1926) and *The Edge of the Unknown* (1930). His *Memoirs and Adventures* appeared in 1924.

Adelheid Kegler is currently researching themes related to the interdisciplinarity of philosophy and literature, with special focus on Neoplatonic imagery in 19th century literature. Other research interests include gnostic elements in the 'landscape of the mind' in paintings, films and literature of the 19th and 20th centuries. Among her publications are essays on the theory of knowledge, ethics and history of consciousness. She has also written on George MacDonald, Emily Brontë, G K Chesterton, C S Lewis and David Lindsay. For more than thirty years she has lectured on philosophy and literature as Director of Studies at a German gymnasium. Several of her curricular topics have been published by the Ministry of Education of Nordrhein-Westfalen.

Gary Lachman is the author of several books on the history and influence of esoteric ideas on western culture including *The Dedalus Book of the Occult: A Dark Muse* (Dedalus, 2003), *In Search of P.D. Ouspensky: The Genius in the Shadow of Gurdjieff* (Quest, 2004) and *The Dedalus Occult Reader: The Garden of Hermetic Dreams* (Dedalus, 2005). He writes frequently for the *Independent on Sunday*, *The Guardian*, and other journals in the UK and US. He is currently working on an introductory volume on Swedenborg entitled *Discovering Swedenborg* to be published by the Swedenborg Society in 2006.

Richard Lines has written a number of articles on Swedenborg's influence on literature, including 'Charles Augustus Tulk: Swedenborgian Extraordinary' (*Arcana*, Vol. III, No. 4, 1997), 'The Inventions of William Blake, Painter and Poet: An Early Appreciation of Blake's Genius' (*The Journal of the Blake Society*, No. 4, 1999) and 'James John Garth Wilkinson: Author, Physician and Translator' (*New Church Historical Society*, 2002). He contributed an entry on J J G Wilkinson for *The Dictionary of Nineteenth-Century British Philosophers* (Thoemmes Press, 2002). His essay 'Swedenborgian ideas in the poetry of Elizabeth Barrett Browning and Robert Browning' was also included in *In Search of the Absolute* (The Swedenborg Society, 2004).

Stephen McNeilly lectures in 'Art and Critical Theory' at the University College for Creative Arts at Canterbury. He has edited a number of books for the Swedenborg Society including *On the Translator and the Latin Text* (2001), *On the True Philosopher and the True Philosophy* (2002), *Introducing the Mystic* by Ralph Waldo Emerson (2003), *Introducing the New Jerusalem* (2003) and *In Search of the Absolute* (2004). He has also edited *x24: An Anthology of Contemporary Poetry* (Black Dog Press, 1997) and is currently editing George Berkeley's *The Commonplace Book* (Dedecus Press, 2006).

W B Yeats (1865-1939) was one of the twentieth century's outstanding literary figures and the winner of the Nobel Prize in 1923. Yeats's verse collections include *The Wind Among the Reeds* (1899), *The Green Helmet and Other Poems* (1910), *Wild Swans at Coole* (1917), *The Tower* (1928) and *The Winding Stair and Other Poems* (1933). A *Collected Poems* was issued in 1933. His plays include *Cathleen ni Houlihan* (1902) and the *Cat and the Moon* (1924), whilst his prose work features *The Celtic Twilight* (1893), *The Secret Rose* (1907) and *A Vision* (1926).

—

Selected Works by Swedenborg

Listed chronologically

Published by Swedenborg

1709	Selected Sentences (*Selectae Sententiae*).
1714	Heliconian Sports (*Ludus Heliconius*).
1715	Northern Muse (*Camena Borea*).
1716-17	Northern Inventor (*Daedalus Hyperboreus*).
1721	On Finding Longitude (*Methodus Nova Inveniendi Longitudines Locorum Terra Marique Ope Lunae*).
	Principles of Chemistry (*Prodromus Principiorum Rerum Naturalium, sive Novorum Tentaminum Chymiam et Physicam*).
1722	Miscellaneous Observations (*Miscellanea Observata*).
1734	The Principia, or Principles of Natural Things (*Principia Rerum Naturalium*).
	The Infinite and the Final Cause of Creation (*Prodromus Philosophiae Ratiocinantis de Infinito, et Causa Finali Creationis*).
1740-2	The Economy of the Animal Kingdom (*Oeconomia Regni Animalis*).
1744-5	The Animal Kingdom (*Regnum Animale*).
1745	The Worship and Love of God (*De Cultu et Amore Dei*).
1749-56	Arcana Caelestia (*Arcana Coelestia*).
1758	Earths in the Universe (*De Telluribus in Mundo nostri Solari*).
	Heaven and Hell (*De Coelo et ejus Mirabilibus, et de Inferno*).

———

The Last Judgment (*De Ultimo Judicio*).

The New Jerusalem and its Heavenly Doctrine (*De Nova Hierosolyma et ejus Doctrina Coelesti*).

The White Horse (*De Equo Albo*).

1763   Doctrine of the New Jerusalem concerning the Lord (*Doctrina Novae Hierosolymae de Domino*).

Doctrine of the New Jerusalem concerning the Sacred Scripture (*Doctrina Novae Hierosolymae de Scriptura Sacra*).

Doctrine of Life for the New Jerusalem (*Doctrina Vitae pro Nova Hierosolyma ex praeceptis Decalogi*).

Doctrine of the New Jerusalem concerning Faith (*Doctrina Novae Hierosolymae de Fide*).

Continuation of The Last Judgment (*Continuatio de Ultimo Judicio*).

Divine Love and Wisdom (*De Divino Amore et de Divina Sapientia*).

1764   Divine Providence (*De Divina Providentia*).

1766   The Apocalypse Revealed (*Apocalypsis Revelata*).

1768   Conjugial Love (*De Amore Conjugiali*).

1769   Brief Exposition (*Summaria Expositio Doctrinae Novae Ecclesiae*).

Interaction of the Soul and Body (*De Commercio Animae et Corporis*).

1771   The True Christian Religion (*Vera Christiana Religio*).

Published Posthumously

1719   On Tremulation (*Anatomi af vår aldrafinaste natur, wisande att vårt rörande och lefwande wäsende består af contremiscentier*).

1734   Mechanism of the Soul and Body (*De Mechanismo Animae et Corporis*).

1738-40   The Cerebrum (*Transactiones de cerebro*).

1738-44   The Brain (*various untitled MS*).

1739   Journeys 1739 (*Mina resors beskrifning*).

1741   Correspondences and Representations (*De Correspondentia et Representatione*).

A Philosopher's Notebook (*Varia Philosophica et Theologica*).

1742   Rational Psychology or The Soul (*Psychologia Rationalis*).

Ontology (*Ontologia*).

Hieroglyphic Key (*Clavis Hieroglyphica*).

1743   The Generative Organs (*De Generatione*).

1743-4   The Journal of Dreams (*Swedenborgs Drömmar*).

1745-7   The Word Explained (*Explicatio in Verbum Historicum Veteris Testamenti*).

1746   Bible Index (*Index Biblicus*).

1747-65   The Spiritual Diary (*Diarium Spirituale*).

1750   Miracles and Signs (*De Miraculis*).

1757-9   The Apocalypse Explained (*Apocalypsis Explicata*).

1759   Athanasian Creed (*De Athanasii Symbolo*).

1760   The Lord (*De Domino*).

1761   Prophets and Psalms (*Summaria Expositio Sensu Interni Librorum Propheticorum ac Psalmorum*).

The Sacred Scripture or Word of the Lord, from Experience (*De Scriptura Sacra seu Verbo Domini*).

1762   Precepts of the Decalogue (*De Praeceptis Decalogi*).

The Last Judgment Posthumous (*De Ultimo Judicio Posth*).

The Divine Love (*De Divino Amore*).

1763   The Divine Wisdom (*De Divina Sapientia*).

1766   Conversations with Angels (*Colloquia cum Angelis*).

Charity (*De Charitate*).

Five Memorable Relations (*Memorabilia*).

Marriage (*De Conjugio*).

1769   Canons of the New Church (*Canones Novae Ecclesiae*).

Scripture Confirmations (*Dicta Probantia*).

Index to Formula Concordiae (*Index ad Formulam Concordiae*).

1770   Ecclesiastical History of the New Church (*Historia Ecclesiatica Novae Ecclesiae*).

1771   Nine Questions (*Quaestiones Novem de Trinitate*).

         Reply to Ernesti (*Responsum ad Dr Ernesti*).

         Coronis (*Coronis seu Appendix ad Veram Christianam Religionem*).

         Consummation of the Age and Invitation to the New Church (*De Consummatione Saeculi, de Adventu Secundo Domini*).

Preface

Stephen McNeilly

For the experience of *correspondances*, Baudelaire refers to Swedenborg.[1]
Walter Benjamin

Man of science, chemist, naturalist, engineer, covered with honours; at fifty-eight: mystical vision, radical transformation [...] new glory: all of Europe becomes interested in him, writes to him, but he doesn't answer.[2]
Roland Barthes

I n 1850, in his famous series of lectures on *Representative Men*, Ralph Waldo Emerson wrote the following lengthy homage to Swedenborg and his significance for Literature:

No one man is able to judge the merits of his works [...] A colossal soul, he lies vast abroad of his times, uncomprehended, requiring a long focal distance to be seen. His superb speculation, as from a tower, over nature and arts, without ever losing sight of the texture and sequence of things, almost realises his own picture of the original integrity of man. Over and above the merit of his particular discoveries, is the capital merit of his self-equality.

One of the missouriums and mastadons of literature, he is not to be measured by whole colleges of ordinary scholars. His stalwart presence would flutter the gowns of any university. Our books are false by being fragmentary: their sentences are *bon mots*, and not parts of the natural discourse; [...] But Swedenborg is systematic and respective of the world in every sentence: all the means are orderly given; his faculties work with astronomic punctuality, and this admirable writing is pure from all pertness or egotism. [3]

Indeed, and as if to confirm Emerson's prediction, few writers over the last 250 years—including Emerson himself—have done more to shape and underpin the hidden currents of modern Literature, influencing writers as diverse as William Blake, S T Coleridge, Honoré de Balzac, Charles Baudelaire, Paul Valéry, Walter Benjamin, George MacDonald, August Strindberg, Robert Browning and Elizabeth Barrett Browning, Coventry Patmore, Fyodor Dostoyesky, Sir Arthur Conan Doyle, Oscar Milosz, W B Yeats, Jorge Luis Borges and Czeslaw Milosz. His name, more recently, has also re-emerged in the work of Italo Calvino, A S Byatt, Peter Ackroyd and Iain Sinclair. Ernst Benz, in 1948, the German historian and biographer of Swedenborg, observed that 'the smallest and least things' in Swedenborg's system offers a 'proclamation of a world higher than itself by reflecting the divine archetype in shadow form like a mirror reflection and silhouette'. [4] In such a way, today, the enormous range and diversity of Swedenborg's appeal leads us to a plethora of approaches and responses, each in some way drawing us closer to an understanding of his work and its particular relevance to writers and poets.

*

The aim of the essays collected here, and in keeping with the previous volume in the series, [5] is to trace a clearer outline of the central stakes of this influence, drawing attention on the one hand to its impact on writers and poets of the 19th and 20th century, and on the other, pointing to themes present in the broader context of Romanticism, Symbolism, Modernism, etc. A further strategy, and drawing on a diverse spectrum of historical research, is to reprint and juxtapose this research with key essays by international authors outlining their own interest in Swedenborg.

The opening essay, as such, and one of the outstanding prose poems of the 20th century, is W B Yeats's 'Swedenborg, Mediums and the Desolate Places'. Originally published in 1920, as a terminal essay to *Visions and Beliefs in the West of Ireland,* [6] Yeats sets the tone for 20th century literary studies of Swedenborg by outlining the central themes of his philosophy in relation to Spiritualism and the hermeneutics of Symbolism, and comparing this to the key tropes of mythology and folklore. Along with Jacob Boehme and William Blake, he suggests, Swedenborg occupies a privileged position in modern literature insofar as he offers a unique means of penetrating the opaqueness of experience through symbols and metaphors.

The second and third articles, by Gary Lachman and Adelheid Kegler respectively, continue the discussion of Swedenborg's influence on Symbolism but with reference to the work of Charles Baudelaire and George MacDonald. Lachman begins with a comparison of Swedenborg's Science of Correspondences and Baudelaire's famous poem 'Les correspondances', and suggests that in conjunction with E T A Hoffman and Edgar Allan Poe, it was Swedenborg who offered to Symbolism its semiotic methodology. Adelheid Kegler, in turn, drawing attention to the use of pictorial landscapes in art and literature, offers a meditation on the short stories of Sheridan Le Fanu and the phantasy writing of George MacDonald. The influence of Swedenborg is of special interest here, she writes, because he offers a model of the mind in spatial terms. Subsequent symbolists have continued to make use of such landscape motifs via complex signs, a methodology, she suggests, which can be seen in the films of Jim Jarmusch and David Lynch.

The fourth article by Richard Lines shifts the focus of enquiry to a study of Swedenborg's influence on Victorian Poetry, and in particular the work of Coventry Patmore. Once one of the most famous and widely read poets of the 19th century—an associate of Gerard Manley Hopkins and the Pre-Raphaelites—Lines argues for a re-evaluation of Patmore's work insofar as it draws on Swedenborg's discussion of gender and sexuality as found in the book *Conjugial Love*. The theme of *Conjugial Love* and poetry is approached again in the following article via an analysis of the mystical poetry of Oscar V de L Milosz, the uncle of the Nobel prizewinning author Czeslaw Milosz. Here, Gary Lachman, in his second essay, leads the reader through an enquiry of the key works of Milosz's writing, drawing out recurring motifs and themes connected with the broader themes of modernist poetry and mysticism.

The final essay in the volume—and along with W B Yeats's 'Swedenborg, Mediums and the Desolate Places', one of the seminal papers of the 20th century on Swedenborg—

is Sir Arthur Conan Doyle's 'The Story of Swedenborg'. First printed in 1926, in *The History of Spiritualism*[7] Conan Doyle outlines his interest in Swedenborg and argues for a closer connection between the organizations formed in the wake of Swedenborg's publications. In keeping with Yeats, he suggests that Swedenborg should be placed at the head of the esoteric and spiritualist tradition, and in his discussion outlines his broader interests in the occult and mysticism earlier hinted at in the Sherlock Holmes stories and in other fictional works. Along with the opening essay in this volume this article is published here with new footnote references.

NOTES

[1] Walter Benjamin, *The Arcades Project*, tr. H Eiland and K McLaughlin (Cambridge, MA: Harvard University Press, 2002 repr.), p. 250. The spelling of *correspondances* here, refers to Baudelaire's famous poem 'Les correspondances'. The full quotation is 'For the experience of *correspondances*, Baudelaire refers to Swedenborg and hashish'.

[2] Roland Barthes, *The Neutral. Lecture Course at the College de France (1977-1978)*, tr. Rosalind E Krauss and Denis Hollier (New York: Columbia University Press, 2005), p.140. This quotation is from the section entitled 'Retreat' where Barthes discusses Swedenborg's 1745 vision at the Inn as an example of the binary relation between internal and external spaces. In the subsequent section he goes on to compare this internal space of Swedenborg's with that of Proust and outlines a typology of the retreat as an arena into which one 'retires'.

[3] Ralph Waldo Emerson, *Emerson on Swedenborg: introducing the Mystic* (London: The Swedenborg Society, 2003), pp. 10-11, a reprint of the essay on Swedenborg as contained in *Representative Men: Seven Lectures* (Cambridge, MA: Harvard University Press, 1996).

[4] Ernst Benz, *Emanuel Swedenborg: Visionary Savant in the Age of Reason*, tr. Nicholas Goodrick-Clarke (West Chester: The Swedenborg Foundation, 2002), p. 352.

[5] *In Search of the Absolute—Essays on Swedenborg and Literature*, containing essays on S T Coleridge, R W Emerson, Walt Whitman, August Strindberg, the Brownings and Jorge Luis Borges (London: Swedenborg Society, 2004).

[6] *Visions and Beliefs in the West of Ireland*, collected by Lady Gregory, 2 vols. (New York: Putnam's, 1920).

[7] Arthur Conan Dole, *The History of Spiritualism*, vol. I (London, 1926).

Essays on Swedenborg
and Literature

Swedenborg, Mediums and the Desolate Places

W B Yeats

I

Some fifteen years ago I was in bad health and could not work, and Lady Gregory brought me from cottage to cottage while she began to collect the stories in this book,[1] and presently when I was at work again she went on with her collection alone till it grew to be, so far as I know, the most considerable book of its kind. Except that I had heard some story of 'The Battle of the Friends'[2] at Aran and had divined that it might be the legendary common accompaniment of death, she was not guided by any theory of mine, but recorded what came, writing it out at each day's end and in the country dialect. It was at this time mainly she got the knowledge of words that makes her little comedies of country life so beautiful and so amusing. As that ancient system of belief unfolded before us, with unforeseen probabilities and plausibilities, it was as though we had begun to live in a dream, and one day Lady Gregory said to me when we had passed an old man in the wood: 'That old man may know the secret of the ages'.

I had noticed many analogies in modern spiritism and began a more careful comparison, going a good deal to séances for the first time and reading all writers of any reputation I could find in English or French. I found much that was moving, when I had climbed to the top storey of some house in Soho or Holloway, and, having paid my shilling,

1

awaited, among servant girls, the wisdom of some fat old medium. That is an absorbing drama, though if my readers begin to seek it they will spoil it, for its gravity and simplicity depends on all, or all but all, believing that their dead are near.

I did not go there for evidence of the kind the Society for Psychical Research would value,[3] any more than I would seek it in Galway or in Aran. I was comparing one form of belief with another, and like Paracelsus, who claimed to have collected his knowledge from midwife and hangman, I was discovering a philosophy.[4] Certain things had happened to me when alone in my own room which had convinced me that there are spiritual intelligences which can warn us and advise us, and, as Anatole France has said, if one believes that the Devil can walk the streets of Lisbon, it is not difficult to believe that he can reach his arm over the river and light Don Juan's cigarette.[5] And yet I do not think I have been easily convinced, for I know we make a false beauty by a denial of ugliness and that if we deny the causes of doubt we make a false faith, and that we must excite the whole being into activity if we would offer to God what is, it may be, the one thing germane to the matter, a consenting of all our faculties. Not but that I doubt at times, with the animal doubt of the Middle Ages that I have found even in pious countrywomen when they have seen some life come to an end like the stopping of a clock, or that all the perceptions of the soul, or the weightiest intellectual deductions, are not at whiles but a feather in the daily show.

I pieced together stray thoughts written out after questioning the familiar of a trance medium or automatic writer, by Allan Kardec, or by some American, or by myself, or arranged the fragments into some pattern, till I believed myself the discoverer of a vast generalization. I lived in excitement, amused to make Holloway interpret Aran, and constantly comparing my discoveries with what I have learned of mediaeval tradition among fellow students, with the reveries of a Neoplatonist, of a seventeenth-century Platonist, of Paracelsus or a Japanese poet. Then one day I opened *The Spiritual Diary* of Swedenborg, which I had not taken down for twenty years, and found all there, even certain thoughts I had not set on paper because they had seemed fantastic from the lack of some traditional foundation. It was strange I should have forgotten so completely a writer I had read with some care before the fascination of Blake and Boehme had led me away.

II

It was indeed Swedenborg who affirmed for the modern world, as against the abstract reasoning of the learned, the doctrine and practice of the desolate places, of shepherds and of midwives, and discovered a world of spirits where there was a scenery like that of earth, human forms, grotesque or beautiful, senses that knew pleasure and pain, marriage and war, all that could be painted upon canvas, or put into stories to make one's hair stand up. He had mastered the science of his time, he had written innumerable scientific works in Latin, had been the first to formulate the nebular hypothesis and wrote a cold abstract style, the result it may be of preoccupation with stones and metals, for he had been assessor of mines to the Swedish Government, and of continual composition in a dead language.

In his fifty-eighth year he was sitting in an inn in London, where he had gone about the publication of a book, when a spirit appeared before him who was, he believed, Christ himself, and told him that henceforth he could commune with spirits and angels. From that moment he was a mysterious man describing distant events as if they were before his eyes, and knowing dead men's secrets, if we are to accept testimony that seemed convincing to Immanuel Kant. The sailors who carried him upon his many voyages spoke of the charming of the waves and of favouring winds that brought them sooner than ever before to their journey's end, and an ambassador described how a queen, he himself looking on, fainted when Swedenborg whispered in her ear some secret known only to her and to her dead brother.[6] And all this happened to a man without egotism, without drama, without a sense of the picturesque, and who wrote a dry language, lacking fire and emotion, and who to William Blake seemed but an arranger and putter away of the old Church, a Samson shorn by the churches, an author not of a book, but of an index.[7] He considered heaven and hell and God, the angels, the whole destiny of man, as if he were sitting before a large table in a Government office putting little pieces of mineral ore into small square boxes for an assistant to pack away in drawers.

All angels were once men, he says, and it is therefore men who have entered into what he calls the Celestial State and become angels, who attend us immediately after death, and communicate to us their thoughts, not by speaking, but by looking us in the face as they sit beside the head of our body. When they find their thoughts are communicated they know the time has come to separate the spiritual from the physical body. If a man begins to feel that he can endure them no longer, as he doubtless will, for in their presence he can think and feel but sees nothing, lesser angels who belong to truth more than to love take their place and he is in the light again, but in all likelihood these angels also will be too high and he will slip from state to state until he finds himself after a few days 'with those who are in accord with his life in the world; with them he finds his life, and, wonderful to relate, he then leads a life similar to that he led in the world'.[8] This first state of shifting and readjustment seems to correspond with a state of sleep more modern seers discover to follow upon death. It is characteristic of his whole religious system, the slow drifting of like to like. Then follows a period which may last but a short time or many years, while the soul lives a life so like that of the world that it may not even believe that it has died, for 'when what is spiritual touches and sees what is spiritual the effect is the same as when what is natural touches what is natural'.[9] It is the other world of the early races, of those whose dead are in the rath or the faery hill, of all who see no place of reward and punishment but a continuance of this life, with cattle and sheep, markets and war. He describes what he has seen, and only partly explains it, for, unlike science which is founded upon past experience, his work, by the very nature of his gift, looks for the clearing away of obscurities to unrecorded experience. He is revealing something and that which is revealed, so long as it remains modest and simple, has the same right with the child in the cradle to put off to the future the testimony of its worth. This earth-resembling life is the creation of the image-making power of the mind, plucked naked from the body, and mainly of the images in the memory. All our work has gone with us, the books we have written can be opened and read or put away for later use, even though their print and paper have been sold to the buttermen; and reading his description one notices, a discovery one had thought peculiar to the last generation, that the 'most minute particulars which enter the memory remain there and are never obliterated',[10] and there as here we do not always know all that is in our memory, but at need angelic spirits who act upon us there as here, widening and deepening the consciousness at will, can draw forth all the past, and make us live again all our transgressions and see our victims 'as if they were present, together with the place, words, and motives'; and that suddenly, 'as when a scene bursts upon the sight' and yet continues 'for hours together',[11] and like the transgressions, all the pleasure and pain of sensible life awaken again and again, all our passionate events rush up about us and not as seeming imagination, for imagination is now the world. And yet another impulse comes and goes, flitting through all, a preparation for the spiritual abyss, for out of the celestial world, immediately beyond the world of form, fall certain seeds as it were that exfoliate through us into forms, elaborate scenes, buildings, alterations of form that are related by 'correspondence' or 'signature' to celestial incomprehensible realities. Meanwhile those who have loved or fought see one another in the unfolding of a dream, believing it may be that they wound one another or kill one another, severing arms or hands, or that their lips are joined in a kiss, and the countryman has need but of Swedenborg's keen ears and eagle sight to hear a noise of swords in the empty valley, or to meet the old master hunting with all his hounds upon the stroke of midnight among the moonlit fields. But gradually we begin to change and possess only those memories we have related to our emotion or our thought; all that was accidental or habitual dies away and we begin an active present life, for apart from that calling up of the past we are not punished or rewarded for our actions when in the world but only for what we do when out of it. Up till now we have disguised our real selves and those who have lived well for fear or favour have walked with holy men and women, and the wise man and the dunce have been associated in common learning, but now the ruling love has begun to remake circumstance and our body.

Swedenborg had spoken with shades that had been learned Latinists, or notable Hebrew scholars, and found, because they had done everything from the memory and nothing from thought and emotion, they had become but simple men.[12] We have already met our friends, but if we were to meet them now for the first time we should not recognize them, for all has been kneaded up anew, arrayed in order and made one piece. 'Every man has many loves, but still they all have reference to his ruling love and make one with it or together compose it',[13] and our surrender to that love, as to supreme good, is no new thought, for Villiers de l'Isle Adam quotes Thomas Aquinas as having said, 'Eternity is the possession of one's self, as in a single moment'.[14] During the fusing and rending man flits, as it were, from one flock of the dead to another, seeking always those who are like himself, for as he puts off disguise he becomes unable to endure what is unrelated to his love, even becoming insane among things that are too fine for him.

So heaven and hell are built always anew and in hell or heaven all do what they please and all are surrounded by scenes and circumstances which are the expression of their natures and the creation of their thought. Swedenborg because he belongs to an eighteenth century not yet touched by the romantic revival feels horror amid rocky uninhabited places, and so believes that the evil are in such places while the good are amid smooth grass and garden walks and the clear sunlight of Claude Lorraine. He describes all in matter-of-fact words, his meeting with this or that dead man, and the place where he found him, and yet we are not to understand him literally, for space as we know it has come to an end and a difference of state has begun to take its place, and wherever a spirit's thought is, the spirit cannot help but be. Nor should we think of spirit as divided from spirit, as men are from each other, for they share each other's thoughts and life, and those whom he has called celestial angels, while themselves mediums to those above, commune with men and lower spirits, through orders of mediatorial spirits, not by a conveyance of messages, but as though a hand were thrust with a hundred gloves,[15] one glove outside another, and so there is a continual influx from God to man. It flows to us through the evil angels as through the good, for the dark fire is the perversion of God's life and the evil angels have their office in the equilibrium that is our freedom, in the building of that fabulous bridge made out of the edge of a sword.

To the eyes of those that are in the high heaven 'all things laugh, sport, and live',[16] and not merely because they are beautiful things but because they arouse by a minute correspondence of form and emotion the heart's activity, and being founded, as it were, in this changing heart, all things continually change and shimmer. The garments of all befit minutely their affections, those that have most wisdom and most love being the most nobly garmented, in ascending order from shimmering white, through garments of many colours and garments that are like flame, to the angels of the highest heaven that are naked.

In the west of Ireland the country people say that after death every man grows upward or downward to the likeness of thirty years, perhaps because at that age Christ began his ministry, and stays always in that likeness; and these angels move always towards 'the springtime of their life' and grow more and more beautiful, 'the more thousand years they live', and women who have died infirm with age, and yet lived in faith and charity, and true love towards husband or lover, come 'after a succession of years' to an adolescence that was not in Helen's Mirror, 'for to grow old in heaven is to grow young'.[17]

There went on about Swedenborg an intermittent 'Battle of the Friends' and on certain occasions had not the good fought upon his side, the evil troop, by some carriage accident or the like would have caused his death, for all associations of good spirits have an answering mob, whose members grow more hateful to look on through the centuries.

Their faces in general are horrible, and empty of life like corpses, those of some are black, of some fiery like torches, of some hideous with pimples, boils, and ulcers; with many no face appears, but in its place a something hairy or bony, and in some one can but see the teeth. [18]

And yet among themselves they are seeming men and but show their right appearance when the light of heaven, which of all things they most dread, beats upon them; and seem to live in a malignant gaiety, and they burn always in a fire that is God's love and wisdom, changed into their own hunger and misbelief.

III

In Lady Gregory's stories there is a man who heard the newly dropped lambs of faery crying in November, [19] and much evidence to show a topsy-turvydom of seasons, our spring being their autumn, our winter their summer, and Mary Battle, my Uncle George Pollexfen's old servant, was accustomed to say that no dream had a true meaning after the rise of the sap; and Lady Gregory learned somewhere on Slieve Ochte that if one told one's dreams to the trees fasting the trees would wither. [20] Swedenborg saw some like opposition of the worlds, for what hides the spirits from our sight and touch, as he explains, is that their light and heat are darkness and cold to us and our light and heat darkness and cold to them, but they can see the world through our eyes and so make our light their light. He seems however to warn us against a movement whose philosophy he announced or created, when he tells us to seek no conscious intercourse with any that fall short of the celestial rank. At ordinary times they do not see us or know that we are near, but when we speak to them we are in danger of their deceits. 'They have a passion for inventing', and do not always know that they invent.

It has been shown me many times that the spirits speaking with me did not know but that they were the men and women I was thinking of; neither did other spirits know me contrary. Thus yesterday and today one known of me in life was personated. The personation was so like him in all respects, so far as known to me, that nothing could be more like. For there are genera and species of spirits of similar faculty (? as the dead whom we seek), and when like things are called up in the memory of men and so are represented to them they think they are the same persons. At other times they enter into the fantasy of other spirits and think that they are them, and sometimes they will even believe themselves to be the Holy Spirit [...][21]

and as they identify themselves with a man's affection or enthusiasm they may drive him to ruin, and even an angel will join himself so completely to a man that he scarcely knows 'that he does not know of himself what the man knows',[22] and when they speak with a man they can but speak in that man's mother tongue, and this they can do without taking thought, for 'it is almost as when a man is speaking and thinks nothing about his words'.[23] Yet when they leave the man 'they are in their own angelical or spiritual language and know nothing of the language of the man'. They are not even permitted to talk to a man from their own memory for did they do so the man would not know 'but that the things he would then think were his when yet they would belong to the spirit',[24] and it is these sudden memories occurring sometimes by accident, and without God's permission that gave the Greeks the idea they had lived before. They have bodies as plastic as their minds that flow so readily into the mould of ours and he remembers having seen the face of a spirit change continuously and yet keep always a certain generic likeness. It had but run through the features of the individual ghosts of the fleet it belonged to, of those bound into the one mediatorial communion.[25]

He speaks too, again and again, of seeing palaces and mountain ranges and all manner of scenery built up in a moment, and even believes in imponderable troops of magicians that build the like out of some deceit or in malicious sport.

IV

There is in Swedenborg's manner of expression a seeming superficiality. We follow an easy narrative, sometimes incredulous, but always, as we think, understanding, for his moral conceptions are simple, his technical terms continually repeated, and for the most part we need but turn for his 'correspondence', his symbolism as we would say, to the index of his *Arcana Caelestia*. Presently, however, we discover that he treads upon this surface by an achievement of power almost as full of astonishment as if he should walk upon water charmed to stillness by some halcyon; while his disciple and antagonist Blake is like a man swimming in a tumbling sea, surface giving way to surface and deep showing under broken deep. A later mystic has said of Swedenborg that he but half felt, half saw, half tasted the kingdom of heaven, and his abstraction, his dryness, his habit of seeing but one element in everything, his lack of moral speculation have made him the founder of a church,[26] while William Blake, who grows always more exciting with every year of life, grows also more obscure. An impulse towards what is definite and sensuous, and an indifference towards the abstract and the general, are the lineaments, as I understand the world, of all that comes not from the learned, but out of common antiquity, out of the 'folk' as we say, and in certain languages, Irish for instance——and these languages are all poetry——it is not possible to speak an abstract thought. This impulse went out of Swedenborg when he turned from vision. It was inseparable from this primitive faculty, but was not a part of his daily bread, whereas Blake carried it to a passion and made it the foundation of his thought. Blake was put into a rage by all painting where detail is generalized away, and complained that Englishmen after the French Revolution became as like one another as the dots and lozenges in the mechanical engraving of his time, and he hated histories that gave us reasoning and deduction in place of the events, and St Paul's Cathedral because it came from a mathematical mind, and told Crabb Robinson that he preferred to any others a happy, thoughtless person.[27] Unlike Swedenborg he believed that the antiquities of all peoples were as sacred as those of the Jews, and so rejecting authority and claiming that the same law for the lion and the ox was oppression, he could believe 'all that lives is holy', and say that a man if he but cultivated the power of vision would see the truth in a way suited 'to his imaginative energy',[28] and with only so much resemblance to the way it showed in for other men, as there is between different human forms. Born when Swedenborg was a new excitement, growing up with a Swedenborgian brother, who annoyed him 'with bread and cheese advice',[29] and having, it may be, for nearest friend the Swedenborgian Flaxman with whom he would presently quarrel, he answered the just translated *Heaven and Hell* with the paradoxical violence of *The Marriage of Heaven and Hell*. Swedenborg was but 'the linen clothes folded up' or the angel sitting by the tomb,[30] after Christ, the human imagination, had arisen. His own memory being full of images from painting and from poetry he discovered more profound 'correspondences', yet always in his boys and girls walking or dancing on smooth grass and in golden light, as in pastoral scenes cut upon wood or copper by his disciples Palmer and Calvert one notices the peaceful Swedenborgian heaven. We come there, however, by no obedience but by the energy that 'is eternal delight', for 'the treasures of heaven are not negations of passion but realities of intellect from which the passions emanate uncurbed in their eternal glory'.[31] He would have us talk no more 'of the good man and the bad', but only of 'the wise man and the foolish', and he cries, 'Go put off holiness and put on intellect'.[32]

Higher than all souls that seem to theology to have found a final state, above good and evil, neither accused, nor yet accusing, live those, who have come to freedom, their senses sharpened by eternity, piping or dancing or 'like the gay fishes on the wave when the moon sucks up the dew'.[33] Merlin, who in the verses of Chrétien de Troyes was laid in the one tomb with dead lovers, is very near and the saints are far away.[34] Believing too that crucifixion and resurrection were the soul's diary and no mere historical events, which had been transacted in vain should a man come again from the womb and forget his salvation, he could cleave to the heroic doctrine the angel in the crystal made Sir Thomas Kelly renounce[35] and have a 'vague memory' of having been 'with Christ and Socrates';[36] and stirred as deeply by hill and tree as by human beauty, he saw all Merlin's people, spirits 'of vegetable nature' and faeries whom we 'call accident and chance'.[37] He made possible a religious life to those who had seen the painters and poets of the romantic movement succeed to theology, but the shepherd and the midwife had they known him would have celebrated him in stories, and turned away from his thought, understanding that he was upon an errand to their masters. Like Swedenborg he believed that heaven came from 'an improvement of sensual enjoyment', for sight and hearing, taste and touch grow with the angelic years, but unlike him he could convey to others 'enlarged and numerous senses',[38] and the mass of men know instinctively they are safer with an abstract and an index.

V

It was, I believe, the Frenchman Allan Kardec and an American shoemaker's clerk called Jackson Davis, who first adapted to the séance room the philosophy of Swedenborg. I find Davis whose style is vague, voluble, and pretentious, almost unreadable, and yet his books have gone to many editions and are full of stories that had been charming or exciting had he lived in Connaught or any place else, where the general mass of the people has an imaginative tongue. His mother was learned in country superstition, and had called in a knowledgeable man when she believed a neighbour had bewitched a cow, but it was not till his fifteenth year that he discovered his faculty, when his native village, Poughkeepsie, was visited by a travelling mesmerist. He was fascinated by the new marvel, and mesmerized by a neighbour he became clairvoyant, describing the diseases of those present and reading watches he could not see with his eyes. One night the neighbour failed to awake him completely from the trance and he stumbled out into the street and went to his bed ill and stupefied. In the middle of the night he heard a voice telling him to get up and dress himself and follow. He wandered for miles, now wondering at what seemed the unusual brightness of the stars and once passing a visionary shepherd and his flock of sheep, and then again stumbling in cold and darkness. He crossed the frozen Hudson and became unconscious. He awoke in a mountain valley to see once more the visionary shepherd and his flock, and a very little, handsome, old man who showed him a scroll and told him to write his name upon it.

A little later he passed, as he believed, from this mesmeric condition and found that he was among the Catskill Mountains and more than forty miles from home. Having crossed the Hudson again he felt the trance coming upon him and began to run. He ran, as he thought, many miles and as he ran became unconscious. When he awoke he was sitting upon a gravestone in a graveyard surrounded by a wood and a high wall. Many of the gravestones were old and broken. After much conversation with two stately phantoms, he went stumbling on his way. Presently he found himself at home again. It was evening and the mesmerist was questioning him as to where he had been since they lost him the night before. He was very hungry and had a vague memory of his return, of country roads passing before his eyes in brief moments of wakefulness. He now seemed to know that one of the phantoms with whom he had spoken in the graveyard was the physician Galen, and the other, Swedenborg. [39]

From that hour the two phantoms came to him again and again, the one advising him in the diagnosis of disease, and the other in philosophy. He quoted a passage from Swedenborg, and it seemed impossible that any copy of the newly translated book that contained it could have come into his hands, for a Swedenborgian minister in New York traced every copy which had reached America.[40]

Swedenborg himself had gone upon more than one somnambulistic journey, and they occur a number of times in Lady Gregory's stories, one woman saying that when she was among the faeries she was often glad to eat the food from the pigs' troughs.[41]

Once in childhood, Davis, while hurrying home through a wood, heard footsteps behind him and began to run, but the footsteps, though they did not seem to come more quickly and were still the regular pace of a man walking, came nearer. Presently he saw an old, white-haired man beside him who said: 'You cannot run away from life,' and asked him where he was going. 'I'm going home', he said, and the phantom answered, 'I also am going home', and then vanished. Twice in later childhood, and a third time when he had grown to be a young man, he was overtaken by the same phantom and the same words were spoken, but the last time he asked why it had vanished so suddenly. It said that it had not, but that he had supposed that 'changes of state' in himself were 'appearance and disappearance'. It then touched him with one finger upon the side of his head, and the place where he was touched remained ever after without feeling, like those places always searched for at the witches' trials. One remembers 'the touch' and 'the stroke' in the Irish stories.

VI

Allan Kardec, whose books are much more readable than those of Davis, had himself no mediumistic gifts. He gathered the opinions, as he believed, of spirits speaking through a great number of automatists and trance speakers, and all the essential thought of Swedenborg remains, but like Davis, these spirits do not believe in an eternal Hell, and like Blake they describe unhuman races, powers of the elements, and declare that the soul is no creature of the womb, having lived many lives upon the earth. The sorrow of death, they tell us again and again, is not so bitter as the sorrow of birth, and had our ears the subtlety we could listen amid the joy of lovers and the pleasure that comes with sleep to the wailing of the spirit betrayed into a cradle. Who was it that wrote: 'O Pythagoras, so good, so wise, so eloquent, upon my last voyage, I taught thee, a soft lad, to splice a rope'?[42]

This belief, common among continental spiritists, is denied by those of England and America, and if one questions the voices at a séance they take sides according to the medium's nationality. I have even heard what professed to be the shade of an old English naval officer denying it with a fine phrase: 'I did not leave my oars crossed; I left them side by side'.

VII

Much as a hashish eater will discover in the folds of a curtain a figure beautifully drawn and full of delicate detail all built up out of shadows that show to other eyes, or later to his own, a different form or none, Swedenborg discovered in the Bible the personal symbolism of his vision. If the Bible was upon his side, as it seemed, he had no need of other evidence, but had he lived when modern criticism had lessened its authority, even had he been compelled to say that the primitive beliefs of all peoples were as sacred, he could but have run to his own gift for evidence. He might even have held of some importance his powers of discovering the personal secrets of the dead and set up as medium. Yet it is more likely he had refused, for the medium has his gift from no heightening of all the emotions and intellectual faculties till they seem as it were to take fire, but commonly because they are altogether or in part extinguished while another mind controls his body. He is greatly subject to trance and awakes to remember nothing, whereas the mystic and the saint plead unbroken consciousness. Indeed the author of *Sidonia the Sorceress*, a really learned authority, considered this lack of memory a certain sign of possession by the devil, though this is too absolute.[43] Only yesterday, while walking in a field, I made up a good sentence with an emotion of triumph, and half a minute after could not even remember what it was about, and several minutes had gone by before I as suddenly found it. For the most part, though not always, it is this unconscious condition of mediumship, a dangerous condition it may be, that seems to make possible 'physical phenomena' and that over-shadowing of the memory by some spirit memory, which Swedenborg thought an accident and unlawful.

In describing and explaining this mediumship and so making intelligible the stories of Aran and Galway I shall say very seldom, 'it is said', or 'Mr So-and-So reports', or 'it is claimed by the best authors'. I shall write as if what I describe were everywhere established, everywhere accepted, and I had only to remind my reader of what he already knows. Even if incredulous he will give me his fancy for certain minutes, for at the worst I can show him a gorgon or chimera that has never lacked gazers, alleging nothing (and I do not write out of a little knowledge) that is not among the sober beliefs of many men, or obvious inference from those beliefs, and if he wants more—well, he will find it in the best authors.[44]

VIII

All spirits for some time after death, and the 'earth-bound' as they are called, the larvae, as Beaumont, the seventeenth-century Platonist, preferred to call them,[45] those who cannot become disentangled from old habits and desires, for many years, it may be for centuries, keep the shape of their earthly bodies and carry on their old activities, wooing or quarrelling, or totting figures on a table, in a round of dull duties or passionate events. Today while the great battle in Northern France is still undecided, should I climb to the top of that old house in Soho where a medium is sitting among servant girls, some one would, it may be, ask for news of Gordon Highlander or Munster Fusilier, and the fat old woman would tell in Cockney language how the dead do not yet know they are dead, but stumble on amid visionary smoke and noise, and how angelic spirits seem to awaken them but still in vain.

Those who have attained to nobler form, when they appear in the séance room, create temporary bodies, commonly like to those they wore when living, through some unconscious constraint of memory, or deliberately, that they may be recognized. Davis, in his literal way, said the first sixty feet of the atmosphere was a reflector and that in almost every case it was mere images we spoke with in the séance room, the spirit itself being far away. The images are made of a substance drawn from the medium who loses weight, and in a less degree from all present, and for this light must be extinguished or dimmed or shaded with red as in a photographer's room. The image will begin outside the medium's body as a luminous cloud, or in a sort of luminous mud forced from the body, out of the mouth it may be, from the side or from the lower parts of the body.[46] One may see a vague cloud condense and diminish into a head or arm or a whole figure of a man, or to some animal shape.

—

I remember a story told me by a friend's steward in Galway of the faeries playing at hurley in a field and going in and out of the bodies of two men who stood at either goal.[47] Out of the medium will come perhaps a cripple or a man bent with years and sometimes the apparition will explain that, but for some family portrait, or for what it lit on while rummaging in our memories, it had not remembered its customary clothes or features, or cough or limp or crutch. Sometimes, indeed, there is a strange regularity of feature and we suspect the presence of an image that may never have lived, an artificial beauty that may have shown itself in the Greek mysteries. Has some cast in the Vatican, or at Bloomsbury been the model? Or there may float before our eyes a mask as strange and powerful as the lineaments of the Servian's *Frowning Man* or of Rodin's *Man with the Broken Nose.*[48] And once a rumour ran among the séance rooms to the bewilderment of simple believers, that a heavy middle-aged man who took snuff, and wore the costume of a past time, had appeared while a French medium was in his trance, and somebody had recognized the Tartuffe of the Comédie Française. There will be few complete forms, for the dead are economical, and a head, or just enough of the body for recognition, may show itself above hanging folds of drapery that do not seem to cover solid limbs, or a hand or foot is lacking, or it may be that some *Revenant* has seized the half-made image of another, and a young girl's arm will be thrust from the withered body of an old man. Nor is every form a breathing and pulsing thing, for some may have a distribution of light and shade not that of the séance room, flat pictures whose eyes gleam and move; and sometimes material objects are thrown together (drifted in from some neighbour's wardrobe, it may be, and drifted thither again) and an appearance kneaded up out of these and that luminous mud or vapour almost as vivid as are those pictures of Antonio Mancini which have fragments of his paint tubes embedded for the high lights into the heavy masses of the paint. Sometimes there are animals, bears frequently for some unknown reason, but most often birds and dogs. If an image speaks it will seldom seem very able or alert, for they come for recognition only, and their minds are strained and fragmentary; and should the dogs bark, a man who knows the language of our dogs may not be able to say if they are hungry or afraid or glad to meet their master again. All may seem histrionic or a hollow show. We are the spectators of a phantasmagoria that affects the photographic plate or leaves its moulded image in a preparation of paraffin. We have come to understand why the Platonists of the sixteenth and seventeenth centuries, and visionaries like Boehme and Paracelsus confused imagination with magic, and why Boehme will have it that it 'creates and substantiates as it goes'.[49]

Most commonly, however, especially of recent years, no form will show itself, or but vaguely and faintly and in no way ponderable, and instead there will be voices flitting here and there in darkness, or in the half-light, or it will be the medium himself fallen into trance who will speak, or without a trance write from a knowledge and intelligence not his own. Glanvill, the seventeenth-century Platonist, said that the higher spirits were those least capable of showing material effects,[50] and it seems plain from certain Polish experiments that the intelligence of the communicators increases with their economy of substance and energy. Often now among these faint effects one will seem to speak with the very dead. They will speak or write some tongue that the medium does not know and give correctly their forgotten names, or describe events one only verifies after weeks of labour.[51] Here and there amongst them one discovers a wise and benevolent mind that knows a little of the future and can give good advice. They have made, one imagines, from some finer substance than a phosphorescent mud, or cobweb vapour that we can see or handle, images not wholly different from themselves, figures in a gallanty show not too strained or too extravagant to speak their very thought.

Yet we never long escape the phantasmagoria nor can long forget that we are among the shape-changers. Sometimes our own minds shape that mysterious substance, which may be life itself, according to desire or constrained by memory, and the dead no longer remembering their own names become the characters in the drama we ourselves have invented. John King, who has delighted melodramatic minds for hundreds of séances with his career on earth as Henry Morgan the buccaneer, will tell more scientific visitors that he is merely a force, while some phantom long accustomed to a decent name, questioned by some pious Catholic, will admit very cheerfully that he is the devil. Nor is it only present minds that perplex the shades with phantasy, for friends of Count Albert de Rochas once wrote out names and incidents but to discover that though the surname of the shade that spoke had been historical, Christian name and incidents were from a romance running at the time in some clerical newspaper no one there had ever opened.

All these shadows have drunk from the pool of blood and become delirious. Sometimes they will use the very word and say that we force delirium upon them because we do not still our minds, or that minds not stupefied with the body force them more subtly, for now and again one will withdraw what he has said, saying that he was constrained by the neighbourhood of some more powerful shade.

When I was a boy at Sligo, a stable boy met his late master going round the yard, and having told him to go and haunt the lighthouse, was dismissed by his mistress for sending her husband to haunt so inclement a spot.[52] Ghosts, I was told, must go where they are bid, and all those threatenings by the old *grimoires* to drown some disobedient spirit at the bottom of the Red Sea, and indeed all exorcism and conjuration affirm that our imagination is king. *Revenants* are, to use the modern term, 'suggestible', and may be studied in the 'trance personalities' of hypnosis and in our dreams which are but hypnosis turned inside out, a modeller's clay for our suggestions, or, if we follow *The Spiritual Diary,* for those of invisible beings. Swedenborg has written that we are each in the midst of a group of associated spirits who sleep when we sleep and become the *dramatis personae* of our dreams, and are always the other will that wrestles with our thought, shaping it to our despite.[53]

IX

We speak, it may be, of the Proteus of antiquity which has to be held or it will refuse its prophecy, and there are many warnings in our ears. 'Stoop not down', says the Chaldaean Oracle, 'to the darkly splendid world wherein continually lieth a faithless depth and Hades wrapped in cloud, delighting in unintelligible images',[54] and amid that caprice, among those clouds, there is always legerdemain; we juggle, or lose our money with the same pack of cards that may reveal the future. The magicians who astonished the Middle Ages with power as incalculable as the fall of a meteor were not so numerous as the more amusing jugglers who could do their marvels at will; and in our own day the juggler Houdin, sent to Morocco by the French Government, was able to break the prestige of the dervishes whose fragile wonders were but worked by fasting and prayer.[55]

Sometimes, indeed, a man would be magician, jester, and juggler. In an Irish story a stranger lays three rushes upon the flat of his hand and promises to blow away the inner and leave the others unmoved, and thereupon puts two fingers of his other hand upon the outer ones and blows. However, he will do a more wonderful trick. There are many who can wag both ears, but he can wag one and not the other, and thereafter, when he has everybody's attention, he takes one ear between finger and thumb. But now that the audience are friendly and laughing the moment of miracle has come. He takes out of a bag a skein of silk thread and throws it into the air, until it seems as though one end were made fast to a cloud. Then he takes out of his bag first a hare and then a dog and then a young man and then 'a beautiful, well-dressed young woman' and sends them all running up the thread.[56] Nor, the old writers tell us, does the association of juggler and magician cease after death, which only gives to legerdemain greater power and subtlety. Those who would live again in us, becoming a part of our thoughts and passion have, it seems, their sport to keep us in good humour, and a young girl who has astonished herself and her friends in some dark séance may, when we have persuaded her to become entranced in a lighted room, tell us that some shade is touching her face, while we can see her touching it with her own hand, or we may discover her, while her eyes are still closed, in some jugglery that implies an incredible mastery of muscular movement. Perhaps too in the fragmentary middle world there are souls that remain always upon the brink, always children. Dr Ochorowicz finds his experiments upset by a naked girl, one foot one inch high, who is constantly visible to his medium and who claims never to have lived upon the earth. He has photographed her by leaving a camera in an empty room where she had promised to show herself, but is so doubtful of her honesty that he is not sure she did not hold up a print from an illustrated paper in front of the camera.[57] In one of Lady Gregory's stories a countryman is given by a stranger he meets upon the road what seems wholesome and pleasant food, but a little later his stomach turns and he finds that he has eaten chopped grass, and one remembers Robin Goodfellow and his joint stool, and witches' gold that is but dried cow dung.[58] It is only, one does not doubt, because of our preoccupation with a single problem, our survival of the body, and with the affection that binds us to the dead, that all the gnomes and nymphs of antiquity have not begun their tricks again.

X

Plutarch, in his essay on the daemon, describes how the souls of enlightened men return to be the schoolmasters of the living, whom they influence unseen;[59] and the mediums, should we ask how they escape the illusions of that world, claim the protection of their guides. One will tell you that when she was a little girl she was minding geese upon some American farm and an old man came towards her with a queer coat upon him, and how at first she took him for a living man. He said perhaps a few words of pious commonplace or practical advice and vanished. He had come again and again, and now that she has to earn her living by her gift, he warns her against deceiving spirits, or if she is working too hard, but sometimes she will not listen and gets into trouble. The old witch doctor of Lady Gregory's story learned his cures from his dead sister whom he met from time to time, but especially at Hallowe'en, at the end of the garden, but he had other helpers harsher than she, and once he was beaten for disobedience.[60]

Reginald Scot gives a fine plan for picking a guide.[61] You promise some dying man to pray for the repose of his soul if he will but come to you after death and give what help you need, while stories of mothers who come at night to be among their orphan children are as common among spiritists as in Galway or in Mayo. A French servant girl once said to a friend of mine who helped her in some love affair: 'You have your studies, we have only our affections'; and this I think is why the walls are broken less often among us than among the poor. Yet according to the doctrine of Soho and Holloway and in Plutarch, those studies that have lessened in us the sap of the world may bring to us good learned, masterful men who return to see their own or some like work carried to a finish. 'I do think', wrote Sir Thomas Browne, 'that many mysteries ascribed to our own invention have been the courteous revelations of spirits; for those noble essences in heaven bear a friendly regard unto their fellow creatures on earth'.[62]

XI

Much that Lady Gregory has gathered seems but the broken bread of old philosophers, or else of the one sort with the dough they made into their loaves. Were I not ignorant, my Greek gone and my meagre Latin all but gone, I do not doubt that I could find much to the point in Greek perhaps in old writers on medicine, much in Renaissance or Mediaeval Latin. As it is, I must be content with what has been translated or with the seventeenth-century Platonists who are the handier for my purpose because they found in the affidavits and confessions of the witch trials, descriptions like those in our Connaught stories. I have Henry More in his verse and in his prose and I have Henry More's two friends, Joseph

___

Glanvill, and Cudworth in his *Intellectual System of the Universe,* three volumes violently annotated by an opposed theologian;[63] and two essays by Mr G R S Mead clipped out of his magazine, *The Quest.* [64] These writers quote much from Plotinus and Porphyry and Plato and from later writers, especially Synesius and John Philoponus in whom the School of Plato came to an end in the seventh century.

We should not suppose that our souls began at birth, for as Henry More has said, a man might as well think 'from souls new souls' to bring as 'to press the sunbeams in his fist' or 'wring the rainbow till it dye his hands'.[65] We have within us an 'airy body' or 'spirit body' which was our only body before our birth as it will be again when we are dead and its 'plastic power' has shaped our terrestrial body as some day it may shape apparition and ghost.[66] Porphyry is quoted by Mr Mead as saying that 'Souls who love the body attach a moist spirit to them and condense it like a cloud',[67] and so become visible, and so are all apparitions of the dead made visible; though necromancers, according to Henry More, can ease and quicken this condensation 'with reek of oil, meal, milk, and such like gear, wine, water, honey'.[68] One remembers that Dr Ochorowicz's naked imp once described how she filled out an appearance of herself by putting a piece of blotting paper where her stomach should have been and that the blotting paper became damp because, as she said, a materialization, until it is completed, is a damp vapour.[69] This airy body which so compresses vapour, Philoponus says, 'takes the shape of the physical body as water takes the shape of the vessel that it has been frozen in',[70] but it is capable of endless transformations, for 'in itself it has no especial form',[71] but Henry More believes that it has an especial form, for 'its plastic power' cannot but find the human form most 'natural', though 'vehemency of desire to alter the figure into another representation may make the appearance to resemble some other creature; but no forced thing can last long'. 'The better genii' therefore prefer to show 'in a human shape yet not it may be with all the lineaments' but with such as are 'fit for this separate state' (separate from the body that is) or are 'requisite to perfect the visible features of a person',[72] desire and imagination adding clothes and ornament. The materialization, as we would say, has but enough likeness for recognition. It may be that More but copies Philoponus who thought the shade's habitual form, the image that it was as it were frozen in for a time, could be again 'coloured and shaped by fantasy', and that it is probable that when the soul desires to manifest it shapes itself, setting its own imagination in movement, or even that it is probable with the help of daemonic co-operation that it appears and again becomes invisible, becoming condensed and rarefied.[73]

Porphyry, Philoponus adds, gives Homer as his authority for the belief that souls after death live among images of their experience upon earth, phantasms impressed upon the spirit body.[74] While Synesius, who lived at the end of the fourth century and had Hypatia among his friends, also describes the spirit body as capable of taking any form and so of enabling us after death to work out our purgation; and says that for this reason the oracles have likened the state after death to the images of a dream.[75] The seventeenth century English translation of Cornelius Agrippa's *De Occulta Philosophia* was once so famous that it found its way into the hands of Irish farmers and wandering Irish tinkers, and it may be that Agrippa influenced the common thought when he wrote that the evil dead see represented 'in the fantastic reason' those shapes of life that are

the more turbulent and furious [...] sometimes of the heavens falling upon their heads, sometimes of their being consumed with the violence of flames, sometimes of being drowned in a gulf, sometimes of being swallowed up in the earth, sometimes of being changed into divers kinds of beasts [...] and sometimes of being taken and tormented by demons [...] as if they were in a dream.

The ancients, he writes, have called these souls 'hobgoblins', and Orpheus has called them 'the people of dreams' saying 'the gates of Pluto cannot be unlocked; within is a people of dreams'.[76] They are a dream indeed that has place and weight and measure, and seeing that their bodies are of an actual air, they cannot, it was held, but travel in wind and set the straws and the dust twirling; though being of the wind's weight they need not, Dr Henry More considers, so much as feel its ruffling, or if they should do so, they can shelter in a house or behind a wall, or gather into themselves as it were, out of the gross wind and vapour.[77] But there are good dreams among the airy people, though we cannot properly name that a dream which is but analogical of the deep unimaginable virtues and has, therefore, stability and a common measure. Henry More stays himself in the midst of the dry learned and abstract writing of his treatise *The Immortality of the Soul* to praise 'their comely carriage […] their graceful dancing, their melodious singing and playing with an accent so sweet and soft as if we should imagine air itself to compose lessons and send forth musical sounds without the help of any terrestrial instrument'[78] and imagines them at their revels in the thin upper air where the earth can but seem 'a fleecy and milky light' as the moon to us,[79] and he cries out that they 'sing and play and dance together, reaping the lawful pleasures of the very animal life, in a far higher degree than we are capable of in this world, for everything here does, as it were, taste of the cask and has some measure of foulness in it'.[80]

There is, however, another birth or death when we pass from the airy to the shining or ethereal body, and 'in the airy the soul may inhabit for many ages and in the ethereal for ever',[81] and indeed it is the ethereal body which is the root 'of all that natural warmth in all generations'[82] though in us it can no longer shine. It lives while in its true condition an unimaginable life and is sometimes described as of 'a round or oval figure'[83] and as always circling among gods and among the stars, and sometimes as having more dimensions than our penury can comprehend.

Last winter Mr Ezra Pound was editing the late Professor Fenollosa's translations of the Noh Drama of Japan, and read me a great deal of what he was doing. Nearly all that my fat old woman in Soho learns from her familiars is there in an unsurpassed lyric poetry and in strange and poignant fables once danced or sung in the houses of nobles. In one a priest asks his way of some girls who are gathering herbs. He asks if it is a long road to town; and the girls begin to lament over their hard lot gathering cress in a cold wet bog where they sink up to their knees and to compare themselves with ladies in the big town who only pull the cress in sport, and need not when the cold wind is flapping their sleeves. He asks what village he has come to and if a road near by leads to the village of Ono. A girl replies that nobody can know that name without knowing the road, and another says: 'Who would not know that name, written on so many pictures, and know the pine trees they are always drawing'. Presently the cold drives away all the girls but one and she tells the priest she is a spirit and has taken solid form that she may speak with him and ask his help. It is her tomb that has made Ono so famous. Conscience-struck at having allowed two young men to fall in love with her she refused to choose between them. Her father said he would give her to the best archer. At the match to settle it both sent their arrows through the same wing of a mallard and were declared equal. She being ashamed and miserable because she had caused so much trouble and for the death of the mallard, took her own life. That, she thought, would end the trouble, but her lovers killed themselves beside her tomb, and now she suffered all manner of horrible punishments. She had but to lay her hand upon a pillar to make it burst into flame; she was perpetually burning. The priest tells her that if she can but cease to believe in her punishments they will cease to exist. She listens in gratitude but she cannot cease to believe, and while she is speaking they come upon her and she rushes away enfolded in flames.[84] Her imagination has created all those terrors out of a scruple, and one remembers how Lake Harris, who led Laurence Oliphant such a dance, once said to a shade, 'How did you know you were damned?' and that it answered, 'I saw my own thoughts going past me like blazing ships'.[85]

In a play still more rich in lyric poetry a priest is wandering in a certain ancient village. He describes the journey and the scene, and from time to time the chorus sitting at the side of the stage sings its comment. He meets with two ghosts, the one holding a red stick, the other a piece of coarse cloth and both dressed in the fashion of a past age, but as he is a stranger he supposes them villagers wearing the village fashion. They sing as if muttering,

We are entangled up—whose fault was it, dear? Tangled up as the grass patterns are tangled up in this coarse cloth, or that insect which lives and chirrups in dried seaweed. We do not know where are today our tears in the undergrowth of this eternal wilderness. We neither wake nor sleep and passing our nights in sorrow, which is in the end a vision, what are these scenes of spring to us? This thinking in sleep for some one who has no thought for you, is it more than a dream? And yet surely it is the natural way of love. In our hearts there is much, and in our bodies nothing, and we do nothing at all, and only the waters of the river of tears flow quickly.

To the priest they seem two married people but he cannot understand why they carry the red stick and the coarse cloth. They ask him to listen to a story. Two young people had lived in that village long ago and night after night for three years the young man had offered a charmed red stick, the token of love, at the young girl's window, but she pretended not to see and went on weaving. So the young man died and was buried in a cave with his charmed red sticks, and presently the girl died too, and now because they were never married in life they were unmarried in their death. The priest, who does not yet understand that it is their own tale, asks to be shown the cave, and says it will be a fine tale to tell when he goes home. The chorus describes the journey to the cave. The lovers go in front, the priest follows. They are all day pushing through long grasses that hide the narrow paths. They ask the way of a farmer who is mowing. Then night falls and it is cold and frosty. It is stormy and the leaves are falling and their feet sink into the muddy places made by the autumn showers; there is a long shadow on the slope of the mountain, and an owl in the ivy of the pine tree. They have found the cave and it is dyed with the red sticks of love to the colour of 'the orchids and chrysanthemums which hide the mouth of a fox's hole'; and now the two lovers have 'slipped into the shadow of the cave'. Left alone and too cold to sleep the priest decides to spend the night in prayer. He prays that the lovers may at last be one. Presently he sees to his wonder that the cave is lighted up 'where people are talking and setting up looms for spinning and painted red sticks'. The ghosts creep out and thank him for his prayer and say that through his pity 'the love promises of long past incarnations' find fulfilment in a dream. Then he sees the love story unfolded in a vision and the chorus compares the sound of weaving to the clicking of crickets. A little later he is shown the bridal room and the lovers drinking from the bridal cup. The dawn is coming. It is reflected in the bridal cup and now singers, cloth, and stick break and dissolve like a dream, and there is nothing but 'a deserted grave on a hill where morning winds are blowing through the pine'.[86]

I remember that Aran story of the lovers who came after death to the priest for marriage.[87] It is not uncommon for a ghost, 'a control' as we say, to come to a medium to discover some old earthly link to fit into a new chain. It wishes to meet a ghostly enemy to win pardon or to renew an old friendship. Our service to the dead is not narrowed to our prayers, but may be as wide as our imagination. I have known a control to warn a medium to unsay her promise to an old man, to whom, that she might be rid of him, she had promised herself after death. What is promised here in our loves or in a witch's bond may be fulfilled in a life which is a dream. If our terrestrial condition is, as it seems the territory of choice and of cause, the one ground for all seed sowing, it is plain why our imagination has command over the dead and why they must keep from sight and earshot. At the British Museum at the end of the Egyptian Room and near the stairs are two statues, one an august decoration, one a most accurate looking naturalistic portrait. The august decoration was for a public site, the other, like all the naturalistic art of the epoch, for burial beside a mummy. So buried it was believed, the Egyptologists tell us, to be of service to the dead. I have no doubt it helped a dead man to build out of his spirit-body a recognizable apparition, and that all boats or horses or weapons or their models buried in ancient tombs were helps for a flagging memory or a too weak fancy to imagine and so substantiate the old surroundings. A shepherd at Doneraile told me some years ago of an aunt of his who showed herself after death stark naked and bid her relatives to make clothes and to give them to a beggar, the while remembering her.[88] Presently she appeared again wearing the clothes and thanked them.

XII

Certainly in most writings before our time the body of an apparition was held for a brief, artificial, dreamy, half-living thing. One is always meeting such phrases as Sir Thomas Browne's 'they steal or contrive a body'.[89] A passage in the *Paradiso* comes to mind describing Dante in conversation with the blessed among their spheres, although they are but in appearance there, being in truth in the petals of the yellow rose;[90] and another in the *Odyssey* where Odysseus speaks not with 'the mighty Heracles', but with his phantom, for he himself 'hath joy at the banquet among the deathless gods and hath to wife Hebe of the fair ankles, child of Zeus and Here of the golden sandals', while all about the phantom 'there was a clamour of the dead, as it were fowls flying everywhere in fear and he, like black night with bow uncased, and shaft upon the string, fiercely glancing around like one in the act to shoot'.[91]

NOTES

[1] 'Swedenborg, Mediums and the Desolate Places' was conceived as an introduction to Lady Gregory's collection of Irish folklore *Visions and Beliefs in the West of Ireland,* 2 vols. (New York: Putnam's, 1920), when the collection was finally published it appeared at the end of the second

volume (pp. 293-339).

[2]WBY describes 'The Battle of the Friends' in his essay 'Away', in *Writings on Irish Folklore, Legend and Myth*, ed. Robert Welch (Harmondsworth: Penguin, 1993), pp. 325-6.

[3]The SPR was established in London in 1882. WBY was an Associate Member of the society from February 1913 to 1928.

[4]Cf. Paracelsus' preface to his *Liber Paragranum*, tr. Franz Hartmann in the latter's *The Life of Philippus Theophrastus, Bombast of Hohenheim, Known by the Name of Paracelsus* (London: George Redway, 1887), p. 18.

[5]Anatole France, 'Romance and Magic', in *On Life and Letters*, tr. A W Evans (London: John Lane, 1914), pp. 306-7.

[6] See Immanuel Kant in his *Dreams of a Spirit-Seer Elucidated through Dreams of Metaphysics* (1766) and a letter to Charlotte von Knobloch, August 10, 1763, both of which can be found in *Kant on Swedenborg: Dreams of a Spirit-Seer and Other Writings*, tr. Gregory R Johnson and Glenn Alexander Magee (Pennsylvania: Swedenborg Foundation, 2002), pp. 42-4 and 69-71 respectively. For the 'charming of the waves' see Christopher Springer's letter to Abbé Pernety, January 18, 1782, in R L Tafel (tr., ed. and comp.), *Documents concerning the Life and Character of Emanuel Swedenborg* (London: Swedenborg Society, 1875-7), vol. II:1, p. 532.

[7]William Blake, *Milton, a Poem in 2 Books* (1804-08), plate 22, l. 50 (p. 506 in *Complete Writings*, ed. Geoffrey Keynes, Oxford: OUP, 1985); and Blake, *The Marriage of Heaven and Hell* (c.1790-3), plate 21 (p. 157 in *Complete Writings*).

[8]See Swedenborg, *Heaven and its Wonders and Hell: from Things Heard and Seen*, tr. Revd James Robson Rendell, rev. F Bayley (Everyman's Library Series, 1909), §§449-51. The quoted phrase is from §450, p. 228.

[9]Cf. ibid., §§498, 452. The quotation is from §461, p. 236.

[10]Cf. ibid., §463, p. 240.

[11]Ibid., §462A, pp. 238-9.

[12]Ibid., §464, pp. 241-2.

[13]Ibid., §477, p. 251.

[14]Villiers de l'Isle-Adam, *Axel*, tr. H P R Finberg (London: Jarrolds, 1925), pt. 1, sc. 6, p. 60.

[15][WBY's note] The Japanese Noh play *Awoi no Uye* has for its theme the exorcism of a ghost which is itself obsessed by an evil spirit. This evil spirit, drawn forth by the exorcism, is represented by a dancer wearing a 'terrible mask with golden eyes'. [*Awoi No Uye* is a play by Ujinobu, for more details see Ernest Fenollosa and Ezra Pound, *'Noh' or Accomplishment: A Study of the Classical Stage of Japan* (New York: Alfred A Knopf, 1917), which contains the text and an introduction to the play. The quoted phrase is a stage direction, ibid., p. 204—ed.]

[16]Swedenborg, *Heaven and Hell*, §489, p. 263.

[17]Ibid., §414, pp. 209-10.

[18]Ibid., §553, pp. 308-9.

[19] Lady Gregory, *Visions and Beliefs*, vol. II, pp. 217-18.

[20] Ibid., vol. I, p. 189.

[21] Cf. Emanuel Swedenborg, *The Spiritual Diary*, tr. George Bush and John H Smithson (London: Swedenborg Society, 2002 repr.), vol. II, §§2860-1, p. 375; and, *Heaven and Hell*, §254, p. 111.

[22] Cf. ibid., §246, pp. 106-7.

[23] Cf. ibid., §266, p. 116.

[24] Ibid., §255, p. 111 and §256, p. 112.

[25] Cf. Swedenborg, *The Spiritual Diary*, §§2203-4, vol. II, p. 181.

[26] Cf. Thomas Lake Harris, *The Wisdom of the Adepts* (Fountain Grove: Privately printed, 1884), §648, p. 263. Swedenborg was never in fact the founder of a church, but the Church of the New Jerusalem is based upon his writings.

[27] Cf. Blake, letter to George Cumberland, April 12, 1827 (p. 878 in *Complete Writings*); Blake, '[Public Address]' (c.1810), Notebook p. 24 (p. 602 in *Complete Writings*); and Henry Crabb Robinson's diary entry for June 13, 1826, in G E Bentley Jr, *Blake Records* (Oxford: Clarendon Press, 1969), p. 332.

[28] Cf. Blake, *A Descriptive Catalogue* (1809), no. v (p. 578 in *Complete Writings*); Blake, *The Marriage of Heaven and Hell* (c.1790-3), plate 22, (p. 158 in *Complete Writings*); ibid., plates 25-7, 'A Song of Liberty' (p. 160 in *Complete Writings*); and Blake, '[A Vision of the Last Judgment]' (1810), Notebook pp. 69-70 (p. 606 in *Complete Writings*).

[29] Frederick Tatham, 'Life of Blake' (MS c.1832) in G E Bentley Jr, *Blake Records*, p. 548.

[30] Blake, *The Marriage of Heaven and Hell*, plate 3 (p. 149 in *Complete Writings*).

[31] Ibid., plate 4 (p. 149 in *Complete Writings*); Blake, '[A Vision of the Last Judgment]', Notebook p. 87 (p. 615 in *Complete Writings*).

[32] Cf. Blake, *Jerusalem*, ch. 4, plate 91, ll. 55-8 (p. 739 in *Complete Writings*).

[33] Blake, *Europe, a Prophecy* (1794), plate 14, l. 3 (p. 243 in *Complete Writings*).

[34] The imprisonment of Merlin is not described by Chrétien de Troyes. WBY's source is William Wells Newell's story 'Niniene', in *King Arthur and the Table Round: Tales Chiefly after the Old French of Crestien of Troyes* (London: A P Watt & Son, 1897), vol. II, pp. 134-9.

[35] WBY means Edward Kelley, the 'skryer' of Royal astrologer Dr John Dee.

[36] See Henry Crabb Robinson's diary entry for December 10, 1825, quoted in G E Bentley Jr, *Blake Records*, p. 310.

[37] Cf. Blake, *A Descriptive Catalogue*, no. iii (p. 570 in *Complete Writings*); Blake, *Jerusalem*, ch. 2, plate 36, ll. 35-7 (p. 663 in *Complete Writings*).

[38] Blake, *The Marriage of Heaven and Hell*, plate 14 (p. 154 in *Complete Writings*); and ibid., plate 11 (p. 153 in *Complete Writings*).

[39] These events are all contained in Andrew Jackson Davis, *The Magic Staff: An Autobiography* (13th edn., Boston: Colby & Rich, 1885).

[40] See Revd George Bush's letters to the *New York Tribune* of November 15, 1846 and August

10, 1847, which have been reprinted in Andrew Jackson Davis, *Memoranda of Persons, Places, and Events* (Boston: William White & Company, 1868), pp. 32-5 and 49-51 respectively.

[41] Lady Gregory, *Visions and Beliefs*, vol. I, p. 175.

[42] Cf. Herman Melville, *Moby Dick; Or, The Whale*, ed. Harold Beaver (Harmondsworth: Penguin, 1975), ch. 98, p. 539.

[43] See William Meinhold, *Sidonia the Sorceress. The Supposed Destroyer of the Whole Reigning Ducal House of Pomerania*, tr. Lady Wilde (London: Reeves and Turner, 1894), vol. I, pp. 59-60.

[44] [WBY's note] Besides the well-known books of Aksakof, Myers, Lodge, Flammarion, Flournoy, Maxwell, Albert de Rochas, Lombroso, Madame Bisson, Delanne, etc., I have made considerable use of the researches of Dr Ochorowicz published during the last ten or twelve years in *Annales des Sciences Psychiques* and in the English *Annals of Psychical Science*, and of those of Professor Hyslop published during the last four years in the *Journal* and *Transactions of the American Society for Psychical Research*. I have myself been a somewhat active investigator.

[45] See John Beaumont, *An Historical, Physiological and Theological Treatise of Spirits, Apparitions, Witchcrafts* (London: Printed for D Browne et al, 1705), ch. I, pp. 3, 14-15.

[46] [WBY's note] Henry More considered that 'the animal spirits' were 'the immediate instruments of the soul in all vital and animal functions' and quotes Hippocrates, who was contemporary with Plato, as saying, 'that the mind of man is [...] not nourished from meats and drinks from the belly but by a clear and luminous substance that redounds by separation from the blood.' Ochorowicz thought that certain small oval lights were perhaps the root of personality itself. [See Henry More, *The Immortality of the Soul* (w.1659), ed. Alexander Jacob (Dordrecht: Martinus Nijhoff Publishers, 1987), book II, ch. XIV, sec. 3, p. 157; and ibid., book II, ch. VIII, sec. 3, p. 126—ed.]

[47] Cf. Yeats, 'Mortal Help', in *Mythologies* (London: Macmillan, 1959), pp. 9-10.

[48] Probably a reference to the Rodin-influenced, Croatian (not Serbian) sculptor Ivan Mestrovic. *The Frowning Man* is a title supplied by WBY.

[49] Cf. Jacob Boehme, *The High and Deep Searching Out of The Threefold Life of Man through The Three Principles* (w. 1620), tr. J Sparrow (London: John M Watkins, 1909 repr.), ch. 6, verse 51, pp. 178-9. See also ibid., ch. 6, verse 2, pp. 164-5.

[50] See Joseph Glanvill, *Saducismus Triumphatus or, Full and Plain Evidence Concerning Witches and Apparitions* (1689), pt. 1, sec. xi (Gainesville, FL: Scholars' Facsimiles & Reprints, 1966), pp. 91-2.

[51] WBY speaks from personal experience. For more details of his investigations see his essay 'Preliminary Examination of the Script of E R', in *Yeats and The Occult*, ed. George Mills Harper (Canada: Macmillan Company, 1975).

[52] Cf. WBY's introduction to the chapter 'Ghosts', in *Fairy and Folk Tales of Ireland*, ed. W B Yeats (Gerrards Cross: Colin Smythe, 1973), p. 117.

[53] Cf. Swedenborg, *The Spiritual Diary*, vol. I, §7, p. 2; also ibid., vol. I, §180, pp. 27-8; ibid., vol. II, §2436, p. 252; and ibid., vol. II, §3181, pp. 476-7.

[54] *The Chaldæan Oracles of Zoroaster*, ed. Sapere Aude, vol. VI of the Collectanea Hermetica series (London: Theosophical Publishing Society, 1845), no. 145, p. 46.

[55] For Robert-Houdin's mission to Algeria see chapters VIII-X of vol. II of his *Memoirs of Robert-Houdin, Ambassador, Author, and Conjuror. Written by Himself*, tr. Lascelles Wraxall (London: Chapmand and Hall, 1859).

[56] This story is found in Lady Gregory, *Gods and Fighting Men: The Story of the Tuatha de Danaan and of the Fianna of Ireland*, w. pref. by W B Yeats (London: John Murray, 1904, repr. 1919), pt. 1, book IV, ch. ix 'Manannan at Play', pp. 108-10.

[57] See Julien Ochorowicz, 'Les Phénomènes Lumineux et la Photographie de l'Invisible', in *Annales Des Sciences Psychiques*, Année 19, July 1909, pp. 193-201.

[58] For the chopped grass see Lady Gregory, *Visions and Beliefs*, vol. II, p. 216; for Robin Goodfellow see Shakespeare, *A Midsummer Night's Dream*, II.i.51-2; and for gold turning into dung see *Visions and Beliefs*, vol. I, pp. 77, 85, 196, vol. II, p. 41.

[59] Cf. *Plutarch's Moralia*, tr. Phillip H De Lacy and Benedict Einarson (London: William Heineman, Cambridge, MA: Harvard University Press, 1959), vol. VII, 'On the Sign of Socrates', sec. 24 (593D-594A), pp. 481-5.

[60] See Lady Gregory, *Visions and Beliefs*, vol. I, pp. 106-7.

[61] Cf. Reginald Scot, *The Discoverie of Witchcraft* (1584), intrd Hugh Ross Williamson (Arundel: Centaur Press, 1964) book xv, ch. viii, p. 334 and book xv, ch. xvii, pp. 352-4.

[62] Sir Thomas Browne, *Religio Medici*, pt. I, sec. 31, in *The Major Works*, ed. C A Patrides (Harmondsworth: Penguin, 1984), p. 99.

[63] Ralph Cudworth, *The True Intellectual System of the Universe,* 3 vols. (London: Printed for Thomas Tegg, 1845). The opposed theologian is Dr J L Mosheim, who published the first Latin translation of the work in 1733 .

[64] The essays are: 'The Spirit-Body: An Excursion into Alexandrian Psycho-Physiology' and 'The Augoeides or Radiant Body', in *The Quest: A Quarterly Review*, vol. I, April 1910 and July 1910 respectively.

[65] Henry More, *The Præexistency of the Soul* (1647), stanza 87, in *Philosophical Poems 1647* (Menston, Yorkshire: The Scolar Press Limited, 1969, facs.), p. 277.

[66] In his *Immortality of the Soul* (1659), Henry More describes the lowest faculty of the soul as the *plastic* or *vegetative* part, which is responsible after death for the manifestation of the spirit. See, for example, book III, ch. 2, sections 1-2, pp. 198-9 and book III, ch. 12, sec. 4, p. 256.

[67] G R S Mead glosses Porphyry (*De Antro Nympharium*, xi) in 'The Spirit-Body: An Excursion into Alexandrian Psycho-Physiology', p. 483. For the corresponding passage in Porphyry, see *On the Homeric Cave of the Nymphs*, in *Select Works of Porphyry*, tr. Thomas Taylor, vol. II of The Thomas Taylor Series (Somerset: The Prometheus Trust, 1999), pp. 150-1.

[68] More, *The Præexistency of the Soul*, stanza 58 (p. 269 in *Philosophical Poems 1647*).

[69] See Ochorowicz, 'Les Phénomènes Lumineux et la Photographie de l'Invisible', p. 201.

———

[70] Mead translates from John Philoponus' *Aristotelis de Anima* in his article 'The Spirit-Body', p. 485.

[71] Mead, 'The Spirit-Body', p. 481.

[72] Cf. More, *The Immortality of the Soul* (1659), book III, ch. V, sections 9-10, pp. 220-1.

[73] John Philoponus, *Aristotelis de Anima*, tr. Mead, in the latter's 'The Spirit-Body', p. 485.

[74] The source for this passage about Homer is not from Philoponus, but from Porphyry's *Comm. in Odyss.*: cf. Mead, 'The Spirit-Body', p. 481 n.2.

[75] Synesius, *On Visions*, 137D, tr. G R S Mead in 'The Augoeides or Radiant Body', pp. 717-18. See also Synesius, *De Insom.*, in *The Chaldæan Oracles of Zoroaster*, ed. Sapere Aude, no. 91, pp. 37-8.

[76] Cf. Henry Cornelius Agrippa von Nettesheim, *Three Books of Occult Philosophy*, tr. J[ohn] F[rench] (2nd edn., London: Chthonios Books, 1987), book III, pp. 479-80.

[77] See More, *The Immortality of the Soul* (1659), book III, ch. III, sections 12-13, p. 209.

[78] Cf. ibid., book III, ch. IX, sec. 4, p. 239.

[79] Cf. ibid., book III, ch. IX, sec. 9, p. 241: 'bounding their sight with such a white faint splendour as is discovered in the Moon'.

[80] Ibid., book III, ch. IX, sec. 4, p. 238.

[81] Ibid., book II, ch. XIV, sec. 7, p. 158.

[82] Ibid., book II, ch. XIV, sec. 3, p. 157.

[83] Cf. ibid., book III, ch. II, sec. 2, p. 199.

[84] The play is called *The Maiden's Tomb*, commonly attributed to Kiyotsugu (1354-1406).

[85] Cf. Thomas Lake Harris, *Appendix to the Arcana of Christianity* (New York: New Church Publishing Association, 1858), p. xi.

[86] The play is *Nishikigi*, by Motokiyo, in *'Noh' or Accomplishment*, pp. 131-49. WBY takes the summary of the play from the preceding chapter, 'Fenollosa on the Noh' (c.1906), pp. 127-30.

[87] See Lady Gregory, *Visions and Beliefs*, vol. I, pp. 122-3.

[88] [WBY's note] Herodotus has an equivalent tale. Periander, because the ghost of his wife complained that it was 'cold and naked', got the women of Corinth together in their best clothes and had them stripped and their clothes burned. [See Herodotus, *The Histories*, tr. Aubrey de Selincourt (Harmondsworth: Penguin Classics, 1954), book V, p. 348——ed.]

[89] Sir Thomas Browne, *Religio Medici*, pt. I, sec. 30 (p. 98 in *The Major Works*).

[90] Dante, *The Paradiso of Dante Alighieri*, ed. and tr. H Oelsner and P H Wicksteed (London: J M Dent, 1899, repr. 1941), XXX, ll. 122-5, p. 371.

[91] Homer, *The Odyssey of Homer*, tr. S H Butcher and A Lang (London: Macmillan, 1879), book XI, ll. 601-8, pp. 190-1.

The Spiritual Detective: How Baudelaire invented Symbolism, by way of Swedenborg, E T A Hoffmann and Edgar Allan Poe

Gary Lachman

I n *Heaven and Hell*, Swedenborg introduced the notion of Correspondences. Although there was a history of similar notions, depicting the relationship between the things of this world and those of the higher, spiritual realms—Jacob Boehme's ideas about the 'signatures of things' and the hermetic dictum that 'as above, so below', for example—Swedenborg's account was generally more detailed and thorough, leaving little ambiguity about his meaning. For Swedenborg, there was a direct, one-to-one link between the elements of our world, both natural and man-made, and the spiritual worlds 'above'. As he writes, 'The whole natural world corresponds to the spiritual world, not only the natural world in general, but also in every particular'. The natural world for Swedenborg meant 'everything in its whole extent that is under the sun'.[1] Just as an effect has its roots in its cause, for Swedenborg, the entire physical world has its being and existence in the spiritual one. And just as a cause may be inferred from its effects, so too the spiritual origin of our world may be inferred from the proper study of its elements. Swedenborg argued that this truth was, at an earlier time, common knowledge, but has long been forgotten. We, people of a later age, have lost it completely, chiefly because of our self-obsession, which draws our attention away from higher matters, and focuses it on earthly, sensual things and the gratification of our appetites. By Swedenborg's time, this drift away from the spiritual and toward the sensual was moving toward its peak. With the rise of science and our increasing dependence on explanation in terms of material causation, the idea that there was some kind of spiritual blueprint for the phenomena of nature, and for human existence as well, was more and more rejected. Today we are, I believe, moving toward a kind of apogee in regard to the spiritual world, with science and popular culture (consumerism) speedily heading to the furthest extreme from any under-standing of a 'higher' reality. Recent years have seen a robust movement in the philosophy of mind, as well as in neuroscience and pharmacology, to 'explain' in physical terms the most spiritual elements of human existence, our consciousness and very selves.[2] And broadly 'metaphysical' sciences, like cosmology and astrophysics—dealing with fundamental questions like the origin of the universe—have been aiming for some time now to arrive at a final 'theory of everything', that would account for reality itself, in terms of purely physical formulae. That other spiritual thinkers, like Rudolf Steiner for example, with his prophecy of an 'Ahrimanic future', voiced similar concerns, suggests that rather than being a purely subjective—or, worse still, aberrant—view of human history, Swedenborg's belief that human consciousness has moved away from an earlier direct perception of the spiritual, deserves careful study.[3]

The course of that movement needs little elaboration; even a cursory familiarity with the history of the last three centuries makes clear that there has been an increasing faith in science as the main bearer of 'truth' for our civilization.[4] Likewise, the details of Swedenborg's Correspondences, fascinating as they are, aren't necessary for an appreciation of this paper—and in any case, the interested reader could do no better than to go to the source itself. Two central ideas, though, are helpful to grasp before we go on. One is that for Swedenborg, as for many thinkers in the western esoteric tradition, the natural world is a kind of *language*. It is something like a series of allegories or hieroglyphics. It is, then, something to be *read*. In a metaphor that will appear again, a forest is not only made of trees: it is also, for Swedenborg, made of *signs*.

Later thinkers will use the term *symbol* rather than *sign*, and this distinction leads to the second idea it will be useful for us to grasp at this point. For Swedenborg, we can say that the direction in which the 'signs' of the natural world point is *vertical*, at least metaphorically. The 'signs' that Swedenborg tells us about 'point', he says, toward the higher, spiritual world.

Now, the 'direction' and 'pointing' I am speaking of are, as I say, metaphorical—and recognizing this reveals a curious fact. Because in trying to explain Swedenborg's notion of Correspondences by using metaphors, I am actually employing the very notion I am trying to explain. Metaphors are terms or expressions that 'stand' for something else; in other words, they show how some things 'correspond' to other things. When I say of a beautiful woman that her face 'bloomed', I mean that the beauty of her face is like that of a rose; in other words, it corresponds to it. The same is true if I say of someone that he 'exploded' with anger. Obviously he didn't literally explode; his anger was so great that its expression 'corresponded' to an explosion.

Now, metaphors make up a large part of our language and speech, so much so that it would be very difficult to convey anything without using them. And it is a curious exercise to go 'metaphor hunting', to become conscious of how many metaphors we use, but are unaware of using. Emerson called language 'petrified poetry', and Nietzsche voiced something very similar when he called everyday speech a series of worn down metaphors, meaning that the phrases and expressions of everyday speech were at one time new and fresh metaphors but have become so commonplace that we no longer recognize them as such. So, in a way, we already know, tacitly, what Correspondences are, and use them all the time. But it is a different and enlightening matter to become aware of them explicitly. Before I go on, I should make clear the distinction between a 'sign' and a 'symbol'. A sign, like a metaphor, 'stands' for something else—and an alert metaphor hunter will notice that, in using the word 'stand', I am using a metaphor to explain what a metaphor does. But there is a difference. A stop sign on the road tells us one thing: that we need to stop at this intersection. It 'stands'—literally, in this case—for the command to stop. Likewise, an exit sign over a door: it tells us that we can leave a room or building in that direction. A symbol, however, is not so specific. A nation's flag can 'stand' for many things: your home, your nation's pride, its laws, its landscapes, and so on. And if we move on to other symbols, like the Christian cross, the Yin-Yang emblem, and other religious icons, we enter an area of much wider scope. Further still, we can speak of symbols in art, in literature, in dreams, in visions and fantasies. These are notoriously difficult to interpret, to pin down (another metaphor) to a specific meaning. So a handy distinction between a sign and a symbol is that with a sign we get greater specificity—a strong connection between the sign and what it stands for—but less *meaning*, and with a symbol we have the opposite: larger scope for *meaning*, but a corresponding vagueness about what it stands for.

As we go on I will try to show how this distinction is related to Swedenborg's 'vertical' Correspondences—which strike me very much as 'signs'—and the more 'horizontal' Correspondences—which strike me as 'symbols'—that the French poet Charles Baudelaire employed in his ideas about art, and which later became the basis for the aesthetic doctrine of Symbolism. The same distinction can be made, I think, between the notion of allegory, which works with a one-to-one correspondence between an image and an abstract idea, and metaphor, which strikes me as a much 'looser' arrangement between meaning and emblem.

We don't know exactly when Baudelaire became aware of Swedenborg's work, or which books of his he read. The first mention of Swedenborg in Baudelaire's writings is in his novella *La Fanfarlo*, which was published in 1847. In it the hero keeps a volume of Swedenborg by his bedside. In the novella, Baudelaire makes no attempt to convey Swedenborg's ideas, and the name is mentioned more or less as a means of creating atmosphere. Baudelaire himself more than likely discovered Swedenborg through reading the novelist Balzac, who, in novels like *Séraphita* and *Louis Lambert* adopts Swedenborg's ideas and uses them to create a framework for the story. It is also possible, as Baudelaire's biographer Enid Starkie suggests, that the poet was familiar with French translations of *Heaven and Hell* and *The Doctrine of the New Jerusalem*, which were available at the time. In fact, Swedenborg's ideas, as well as those of other 'occult' thinkers like Franz Anton Mesmer, were 'in the air' in France at this time, forming part of the philosophical climate of Romanticism, so it's quite possible that Baudelaire 'picked them up' without much direct study of the original texts themselves.

What seems clear from a study of Baudelaire's life is that his interest in Swedenborg coincided with his profound discovery of the works of another poet, Edgar Allan Poe. *La Fanfarlo*, as I said, was published in 1847, and this was the year that Baudelaire first encountered Poe's work. A translation of Poe's story 'The Black Cat' by Isabelle Meunier appeared in the January 1847 issue of *La Démocratie Pacifique*. Baudelaire read this and his discovery of Poe was probably the most important event of his life. During Baudelaire's lifetime his literary reputation rested not on his work as a poet, but on his translations of Poe. Baudelaire felt a profound identification with the American poet; in Poe's work he discovered themes and ideas that he himself had entertained for some time. The 'correspondence', as it were, between Poe and Baudelaire even extended to Baudelaire finding actual sentences in Poe's work that he, Baudelaire, had written, *prior* to even knowing about Poe. Poe indeed became an obsession of Baudelaire's. He questioned everyone he met about the writer and, on one occasion, burst into the hotel room of an American writer who was visiting Paris, and subjected him to an impromptu quiz on Poe's career and standing in American letters. One sign of the effect Poe had on Baudelaire is that, while easily wearied when engaged in his own creative work, when working on his Poe translations, Baudelaire exhibited a diligence and industry that was unusual for him. Baudelaire went on translating Poe for nearly twenty years, wrote two long essays about his life and work as well as several shorter ones, and, as I've said, was associated in the French literary consciousness of the time with the work of the American poet and short story writer.

That association began in 1848 when Baudelaire published the first of his Poe translations, the short story 'Mesmeric Revelations'. What is curious about this story is that it purports to be a factual account of a mesmerist who puts an individual who is at the point of death into a trance, during which the mesmerized subject reports on a variety of 'occult' or metaphysical questions. Poe had a deep interest both in mesmerism[5] and in metaphysics, and the revelations conveyed in the story are a sort of trial run for Poe's longer excursion into cosmology, his 'scientific prose poem', *Eureka*. What is also curious about 'Mesmeric Revelations' is that after its publication, Poe received letters from a Swedenborgian group, thanking him for corroborating Swedenborg's insights about the after world; the group clearly believed that Poe had written a true account. Poe was a notorious trickster, given to literary hoaxing, and, as a professed rationalist, he dismissed such remarks as the praise of fools. Poe himself seems not to have read Swedenborg, or if he did, not to have thought much of him. His knowledge of mesmerism came from a book, *Facts in Mesmerism* (1840), by the Reverend Chauncy Hare Townshend, and it attracted him because of its 'scientific' approach to the phenomena of trance.

At this point, however, it's not important whether or not Poe accepted or even knew of Swedenborg's doctrines; what is crucial is to recognize that for Poe, as for Baudelaire, the poet/writer is a kind of seer, an individual privy to knowledge and insights unavailable to the average person. 'Mesmeric Revelations' conveys this idea directly; it runs, however, throughout all of Poe's work and is, paradoxically, portrayed most clearly in those works in which Poe professed his 'rationalism' most directly, his tales of detection, specifically 'The Purloined Letter'. I say that Poe's notion of the poet as a seer is conveyed most clearly in this story; but, again paradoxically, the fact that this idea is subtly 'hidden'—although it is in reality in open view—is what makes it 'clear'.

This admittedly complicated situation may become more apparent as we go along.

But before we move onto 'The Purloined Letter', there is another writer, whose influence on Baudelaire was as profound as Poe's or Swedenborg's. Before becoming known as a poet, or even as a translator of Poe, Baudelaire had gained a reputation as an art critic. In his *Salon of 1846*, in a section exploring the effects of colour (and which contains a magnificent example of Baudelaire's poetic prose), Baudelaire introduces an idea that will be crucial to his later notion of Correspondences. Remarking on a tavern whose red and green façade was, for Baudelaire's eyes, 'a source of exquisite pain', Baudelaire asks if any 'analogist has drawn up a well authenticated scale of colours and their corresponding feelings'. He then goes on to quote a passage from the German fantasist and critic E T A Hoffmann, in which Hoffmann describes how often, when on the point of sleep, but also while listening to music, he finds 'an analogy and close union between colours, sounds and scents'. 'I have the impression', Hoffmann writes, 'that all these things have been created by one and the same ray of light, and that they are destined to unite in a wonderful concert'. He then goes on to describe how the scent of brown and red marigolds produces 'a magical effect' on his being, easing him into a profound reverie, in which he hears the far off sound of an oboe.[6] Elsewhere, Hoffmann also described his alter-ego, Kapellmeister Johannes Kreisler (the pseudonym he used for some of his critical writings), as wearing a coat that was in C sharp minor, with a collar in E major. And he later wrote that 'It is no empty metaphor, no allegory, when a musician says that colour, fragrance, light appear to him as sounds, and that in their intermingling he perceives an extraordinary concert'.[7]

The phenomenon Hoffmann is describing is known as synesthesia, when one sense is substituted for another: in some unusual psychological states, we see sounds, hear colours, feel tastes, etc. It was a phenomenon known to both Baudelaire and Poe. In his *Marginalia*, Poe remarks that 'The orange ray of the spectrum and the buzz of the gnat (which never rises above the second A), affect me with nearly similar sensations. In hearing the gnat, I perceive the colour. In perceiving the colour, I seem to hear the gnat'.[8] In a note to the poem 'Al Aaraaf', Poe remarks that 'I have often thought I could distinctly hear the sound of the darkness as it stole over the horizon'.[9] Baudelaire himself, just before quoting Hoffmann's remark, speaks of colour in musical terms, commenting on its 'harmony' and 'melody'. In our own everyday speech we adopt similar expressions, calling some colours 'loud' and others 'muted'. Perhaps less frequently, we speak of some tones as 'bright' and others as 'dark'. (Certainly we speak of 'high' and 'low' pitch, ascribing a spatial value to sounds which, if you think about it, seems a bit odd.) Hoffmann, Poe and Baudelaire were not the only artists fascinated by this curious phenomenon. Richard Wagner, another influence on Baudelaire, knew of it, and in 'Richard Wagner and *Tannhauser* in Paris', Baudelaire describes the synesthetic effect of listening to Wagner's music.[10] The painter Wassily Kandinsky employed synesthesia in his work, as did the composers Alexandre Scriabin and Olivier Messiaen, the playwright August Strindberg, the poet Arthur Rimbaud and the novelist Vladimir Nabokov, to name a few.[11]

Like the philosopher Arthur Schopenhauer, Hoffmann believed that music was in some way our most direct link to the higher worlds. Music, he says, is 'a universal language of nature'. It is 'the mysterious Sanskrit of nature, translated into sound'. Only through music can we perceive 'the sublime song of trees, flowers, animals, stones, water'. 'Music', Hoffmann argues when writing of Beethoven, 'reveals to man an unknown realm, a world quite separate from the outer sensual world surrounding him, a world in which he leaves behind all precise feelings in order to embrace an inexpressible longing'.[12]

So, like Swedenborg, Hoffmann also expresses the idea that the visible natural world is a kind of language, a 'Sanskrit', and that for him, music is the key to deciphering its meaning. As in the spectrum, white contains all the other colours, for Hoffmann, music is the primal source of all other phenomena, the 'ray of light' he speaks of in the passage quoted by Baudelaire, that contains everything else, destined to be united again in a 'wonderful concert'. For Hoffmann, the phenomenon of synesthesia is evidence of this. It is also clear that synesthesia is another form of 'correspondence' although, unlike Swedenborg's, it is a less rigorous version. The colour orange 'corresponded' for Poe to the sound of a gnat's buzzing, but the same is not necessarily true for other people. Red and brown marigolds 'corresponded' for Hoffmann to the distant sound of an oboe. Again, although Baudelaire and others (the composer Scriabin, for example) believed that a strict 'scale of analogies' could be devised (Baudelaire believed the effect of Wagner's music on himself and others was evidence of this), it would be surprising if we all heard an oboe when faced with marigolds. This *horizontal* form of correspondence then, between the elements of the sensual world, admits a degree of subjectivity, which, to my mind, shifts the agents of correspondence from being 'signs', as in Swedenborg, to 'symbols'.[13]

Let's return to Poe. I've said that the notion of the poet/writer/artist as seer runs through all of Poe's work, but that it is most clearly expressed, *if we know how to look for it*, in the story 'The Purloined Letter'. Poe was a paradoxical character—not surprising, as most poets, writers or artists are—and while he advances the idea of the artist as seer, he was also eager to present himself as a strictly 'scientific' or 'rational' thinker.[14] The term he uses is 'ratiocination' and he even applied this approach to poetry, writing an essay on 'The Rationale of Verse'. Poe's self-professed aspirations to scientific thinking reached visionary, if flawed, heights in *Eureka*. He was, however, much more successful in embodying those aspirations in a fictional alter-ego, the detective C Auguste Dupin, hero of 'The Murders in the Rue Morgue'—considered the first 'detective story'—'The Mystery of Marie Roget', and 'The Purloined Letter'.

The type of tale Poe originated is out of fashion these days, its place being usurped by the 'crime novel', and although the most famous 'consulting detective' in the world is Conan Doyle's Sherlock Holmes, the average reader may be unaware that one of the models for Holmes was Poe's Dupin. Holmes differs from contemporary private eyes— or police investigators, for that matter, and this in itself is indicative of the change in sensibility—by being somewhat 'eccentric'.[15] He keeps his tobacco in a Persian slipper;

when bored in between cases, he takes cocaine; he plays the violin, etc. These traits place Holmes 'outside' the normal run of things, and the same is true, to an even greater degree, of Poe's Dupin.

Funnily enough, Dupin lives in Paris——that is, for Poe's American readers, he is 'foreign', hence somewhat strange. But his oddness doesn't stop there. According to Poe's unnamed narrator, who appears in each story, Dupin is a somewhat isolated figure, an aristocrat fallen on hard times, a man of a higher nature who is yet destitute of material things. He lives in a 'time-eaten and grotesque mansion' in a 'retired and desolate portion of the Fauberg St. Germain'. The narrator meets Dupin in an obscure library where he discovers they are both in search of the same rare volume. They find that they share a predilection for darkness. Dupin wears coloured spectacles, even at night time (and Poe may be responsible for the practice in some circles of wearing sunglasses after dark), and during the day, Dupin draws all the shutters to his room, preferring to rely on the dim light of a few candles. He meditates in total darkness and smokes a pipe that produces a curious aroma. Dupin is only active during the night, when he leaves his apartment to seek 'that infinity of mental excitement which quiet observation can afford'. He is, naturally, contemptuous of the methods of the police force, yet his *noblese oblige* compels him to offer his services to them when needed. Where the police bungle through a case, using brute force as their preferred method, Dupin relies on his mind, which, for him, provides a greater illumination than gaslight. Although he shrouds himself in darkness, he is yet able to see things that invariably elude the authorities.

This ability to perceive things that the average individual is blind to (although Dupin himself, by normal standards, lives in darkness) is most eloquently portrayed, as I've said, in 'The Purloined Letter'. In the story, an important letter has been stolen from a person in high office; if its contents are made public, there would be profound, catastrophic consequences. Monsieur G, the Prefect of the Paris police, calls upon Dupin for help in recovering the letter. The police know who has stolen the letter, but although they've searched the thief's apartment from top to bottom several times, they've been unable to find it. Poe describes in detail the police procedure, which, in essence, is a method of *analysis*. Basically, the police have *taken apart* and *peered into* everything in the apartment that could possibly serve as a hiding place. Yet they have failed to uncover the document.

Now, although Poe and Dupin pride themselves on being 'scientific', the failure of the police to uncover the missing document through these methods suggests to me that Poe is making a criticism of the scientific 'method' itself. That method is analysis, the taking apart of nature in order to discover her secrets. 'We murder to dissect', as Wordsworth says. Dupin, however, employs other means. On a pretext he visits the apartment of the thief and there uses his superior mind to find the document. He first employs a kind of 'correspondence', by which he imagines himself into the mind of the thief. By adopting the facial expression of the thief, as he engages him in conversation—all the while examining the room, his eyes hidden by his dark glasses—Dupin 'feels' himself into the psyche of his opponent. The thief's facial expression corresponds to his thoughts, an insight we can also find in Swedenborg. 'The nature of correspondence', he writes, 'is visible in man in his face [. . .] all the mind's affections stand out visibly, in a physical form as in their imprint'. By adopting the physical form of the thief's face, Dupin is also able to have his thoughts.[16] In this fashion, Dupin is able to locate the hidden letter, which, it turns out, is not 'hidden' at all, but has been left out on a desk in open view—the last place the police would look. The secret that the police, using the scientific method of analysis, have been unable to discover, is in plain sight to the eccentric detective Dupin—who, he tells us, is 'something' of a poet. And just as the purloined letter is in plain sight, to those *who know how to look for it*, so too is Poe's message: that the poet/writer/artist can see things that the average person, even the scientist, cannot. Poe may present Dupin as a proponent of 'ratiocination', but he is able to discover that which is hidden *in full view*, because he is a poet.[17]

Earlier I said that Swedenborg believed that at an earlier time, the Correspondences between the natural and spiritual worlds were visible to everyone.[18] It is only in recent times that they have become 'hidden', or rather, that our vision has become so clouded with petty and selfish matters that we can no longer see them. The Correspondences themselves remain; it is *our sight* that has deteriorated. Poe, Hoffmann and Baudelaire seem to be telling us that this may be true, but that there is a type of person who can, at least on occasion, still recognize the Correspondences, still read the secret 'Sanskrit' of nature and see that which is 'hidden' to the rest of us. That person is the poet, the writer, the artist. He or she can 'detect' the hidden secret, find what is out of sight to the rest of us, and, what is more, help others to see it as well. This, in essence, is the central theme of Symbolism. The symbolist artist or poet can decode the secret messages of existence. As the critic Anna Balakian writes, 'With his superior network of senses and perceptions, [the poet] is bent on deciphering, rather than conveying or communicating, the enigmas of life'.[19]

In his famous poem, 'Les correspondances', Baudelaire tells us that 'Nature is a temple', a forest through which we pass 'symbolically'. Like the apartment containing the purloined letter, the hidden message of nature is there, in full view, but most of us do not see it. Those who do, the artists, Baudelaire tells us, are like children. Like the child, the artist 'enjoys to the highest degree the faculty of taking a lively interest in things, even the most trivial in appearance'.[20] Baudelaire likens this fresh, innocent appreciation of things to the sensibility of a convalescent and to support this notion, refers to Poe's story 'The Man of the Crowd'. Sitting in a coffee-house in London, Poe's narrator is convalescing after months of illness. Looking out of the window he found himself 'in one of those happy moods which are so precisely the converse of *ennui*—moods of keenest appetency, when the *film from the mental vision departs* [my emphasis] [...] and the intellect, electrified, surpasses [...] its everyday condition'. He feels a 'calm but inquisitive interest in everything',[21] which, if we follow Baudelaire, is shared by children, but also by the 'reader' of life's symbols.

It is curious that the story Baudelaire chooses to emphasize the 'aesthetic' quality of convalescence is one that focuses on the city; in the rest of Poe's tale, his narrator becomes fascinated with a face seen in the crowd, which he follows throughout London for a day. In 'The Painter of Modern Life', and in other essays and poems, Baudelaire argues that not only nature, but the man-made world—'modernity'—is a kind of 'forest' of symbols, and that the poet and artist must learn to 'read' this as well. This idea of 'reading' the city had a great influence on the German-Jewish critic Walter Benjamin, who saw in the incidental, chance occurrences of urban experience, indicators of larger social and historical forces.[22] As nature corresponded to the spiritual world, so did the urban backdrop correspond to social, economic and political powers. Space doesn't allow more than a mention of this, but I think a possible Swedenborg—Baudelaire—Benjamin connection worth considering.

What we can gather from Baudelaire's writings on modernity, is that, like Dupin, the modern artist or poet must not take for granted what others would reject. Like children and convalescents, fascinated with everything, even what is 'the most trivial in appearance', the modern reader of nature's—or the man-made world's—Sanskrit, can discover a beauty and meaning that the rest of us may ignore. Just as there is a unity behind the correspondences of the natural and spiritual worlds, and a unity behind the plurality of senses (as evidenced by synesthesia), Baudelaire believed there was a unity of the arts. The true aim of all poetry, all art, all music was to lead the reader or viewer or listener to this unity, which, for Baudelaire, as for Swedenborg, was a revelation of the higher worlds. Baudelaire shocked the critics of his time by arguing that this revelation could come from the most unlikely source: the shifting, inelegant, anarchic surface of urban life. But like Dupin, who was able to uncover what was hidden in full view, with his Symbolism, Baudelaire was able to find the spiritual where the rest of us may find nothing.

NOTES

[1] Emanuel Swedenborg, *Heaven and Hell*, tr. J C Ager (London: The Swedenborg Society, 1958), pp. 44-5.

[2] For more on the urge to 'explain' consciousness, see the introduction to my *A Secret History of Consciousness* (Great Barrington, MA: Lindisfarne, 2003).

[3] For an account of Steiner's somewhat gloomy prognosis, see my article 'Rudolf Steiner and the Ahrimanic Future', in *Journal for Anthroposophy* (Spring, 1993).

[4] Some readers may wonder how the rise of religious fundamentalism, both in the Christian west and the Islamic middle east, can be explained in terms of an increasing dominance of materialist science. Although both movements are clearly very powerful, they are, it seems to me, reactions to the dominance I am speaking of. Their appearance strikes us as radical and extreme, precisely because both pose a challenge to the reigning rationalist materialist dogma. While that dogma needs to be challenged, it is unfortunate that its most vociferous opponents present alternatives that are equally undesirable.

[5] Poe's other classic mesmerist tales are, of course, 'The Facts in the Case of M. Valdemar' and 'A Tale of the Ragged Mountains'.

[6] Quoted in Charles Baudelaire, *Selected Writings on Art and Literature*, tr. P E Charvet (London: Penguin, 1992), p. 58.

[7] E T A Hoffmann, *E T A Hoffmann's Musical Writings* (Cambridge: CUP, 1989), p. 164.

[8] Edgar Allan Poe, *Essays and Reviews* (New York: Literary Classics of the United States, 1984), p. 1322.

[9] Quoted in Patrick E Quinn, *The French Face of Edgar Poe* (Carbondale: Southern Illinois University Press, 1957), p. 150.

[10] See Baudelaire, *Selected Writings on Art and Literature*, pp. 331-2.

[11] Interest in synesthesia was popular in Baudelaire's day. See Enid Starkie, *Baudelaire* (Harmondsworth: Penguin, 1971), pp. 271-3 for an account of 'smell concerts' and other synesthetic events in the Paris of the 1840s.

[12] Hoffmann, pp. 94, 96.

[13] One approach to correspondences on both the sensual and spiritual planes is that employed in some forms of ceremonial magic. The notorious 'magician' Aleister Crowley devised an elegant and detailed set of correspondences, including colours, scents, astrological signs, magical symbols and much else, based on the Kabbalistic Tree of Life. See his *Liber 777*. Such correspondences were also employed in a similar fashion as a means of maintaining health and well-being by the Renaissance magus Marsilio Ficino. See his *Book of Life*.

[14] In this Poe is very much like his later disciple, the weird fiction writer H P Lovecraft, who professed a strict materialist philosophy, yet wrote tales of supernatural and occult horror.

[15] Whereas the detective tale began with individuals who worked *outside* the law and were in many ways superior to the police (who, having failed to solve the case, turned to the amateur sleuth for help), today's dreary but obligatory 'realism' demands as 'factual' and quotidian a narrative as possible. Sherlock Holmes is a kind of superman, solving mysteries beyond the powers of the authorities; police procedural novels and television programs plod on through every minute detail of often boring work. A further decline is evidenced in the popularity of 'real crime' programs, which jettison the idea of story altogether, and aim a video camera at cops on the beat.

[16] In explaining his methods to his companion, Dupin also makes the very Swedenborgian remark that 'The material world . . . abounds with very strict analogies to the immaterial'. Edgar Allan Poe, *Selected Writings* (Harmondsworth: Penguin, 1984), p. 344.

[17] It is curious to recall that in the story Monsieur G reminds Dupin that the thief, Minister D——, is 'a poet'. Poe may also be saying that it takes a poet to find what another poet has hidden, meaning that only one poet can understand the work of another.

[18] There is evidence to suggest that in the first few months of life, children experience the world synesthetically, that is, their experience of the world is not yet refracted into the different sensory modes. There is also some reason to believe that early humans had a very similar mode of experience. For more on synesthesia and its relation to the evolution of consciousness, see

my chapter 'Hypnagogia', in *A Secret History of Consciousness*.

[19] Anna Balakian, *The Symbolist Movement* (New York: New York University Press, 1977), p. 47.

[20] Baudelaire, *Selected Writings on Art and Literature*, p. 398.

[21] Edgar Allan Poe, *Selected Writings*, p. 179.

[22] See Benjamin's essay 'On Some Motifs in Baudelaire', in *Illuminations* (London: Fontana Press, 1992), pp. 152-96.

Elements of Swedenborgian Thought in Symbolist Landscapes: with reference to Sheridan Le Fanu and George MacDonald

Adelheid Kegler

> I have it in me so much nearer home
> To scare myself with my own desert places
> ——Robert Frost

For the narrator of Sheridan Le Fanu's 'Judge Harbottle'——the famous Dr Hesselius introduced in the story's prologue——there is only one account describing the fate of the Honourable Mr Justice Harbottle, an infamous and brutal judge of the late 18th century. This account is discussed as the lesser of two, the other having been lost in mysterious circumstances.

The 'twist' that defines the fate of the judge begins with an everyday situation. The judge is waiting in his carriage for two acquaintances whom he has invited out to dinner. Time passes and the judge, annoyed, falls asleep. Eventually, the coach begins to move. After an unusually long drive, the judge at last gives the order to stop. A glance out of the coach window shows him far from his expected surroundings:

> [...] through the windows, under a broad moonlight, he saw a black moor stretching lifelessly from right to left, with rotting trees, pointing fantastic branches in the air, standing here and there in groups, as if they held up their arms on twigs like fingers in terrible glee at the Judge's coming. [1]

And if this haunting scene is not enough, instead of his accustomed servant the judge sees the ghost of his former footman, a man who, consequent of his judgment some fifteen years previously, had perished in prison. Eventually, the carriage halts before an enormous three-armed gallows. Hanging from the beams of the gallows are skeletons, still in their chains, dangling in the wind. A long ladder stretches from floor to beam.

The reader might think this scene is merely an episode from a good ghost story and characteristic of the works of Sheridan Le Fanu. The motifs and images deployed, however, are more than mere semblances ('only seem'). A court of judgment, which 'never rose day or night',[2] takes place under a ghostly presiding Judge, a giant image of Judge Harbottle himself. And the pronouncement of the judge is one of 'Guilty', an eternal judgment. The doubling of the figure of the judge is a device, a motif directed to opening the 'reader's eyes': the whole story leading the reader to 'an opening of the interior sense',[3] as Dr Hesselius enigmatically remarks in his prologue. Le Fanu's story, as such, is a parable, Swedenborgian in emphasis, which is concerned with revealing a *judgment* of the inner human character before God:

> In the light of the higher world, each person appears revealed as he really is and as his inner memory portrays him. [...] No extrinsic judge rules on the person, but each carries his or her own judge within.[4]

The ladder, leaning on the gallows, points towards Harbottle's inevitable fate, a condemnation which unfolds, step by step, throughout the story. The ghostly setting in the foreground, likewise—the black moor which stretches out lifelessly, the rotting trees with their raised branches and twigs (accusing and triumphant and looking like arms and fingers)—offers more than mere atmospheric effect: it represents a pictorial manifestation of the judge's own soul-landscape, his 'mental landscape'.[5]

This 'mental landscape' represented as an image of nature expresses both a universal and an individual state of consciousness. It is a key—again both particular and general—as to how experience is comprehended. For instance, with regard to the early days of humankind, the 'mental landscape' of the ice-age hunter can be represented as a cave, interpreted as the womb of the Earth-Mother in drawings and accentuations on the walls of caves, and so on. Initiation here means understanding oneself as a child of the Great Mother and a sibling of her other children, born and reborn in a sacred cyclical rhythm. The 'mental landscape' of modern man, in contrast, is of a movement whose direction is uncertain, characterized by darkness; a 'floating darkness' in David Lynch's words. In Judge Harbottle's case, his individual consciousness is literally floating into darkness. It is a 'mental landscape' with no experience of depth.

A related image giving insight into this complex inner structure—but represented by a portrait—can be seen in a painting by George Frederick Watts entitled *The Dweller in the Innermost*.[6] The observer of the painting sees a winged, female figure sitting in a contemplative position. Chin and cheek are held lightly in the left hand.[7] At first glance she seems to be looking straight at the observer. However, on closer inspection, we notice her gaze is also directed elsewhere, towards something lying further behind or beyond. She is surrounded by dense, wafting, orange clouds as if by a mandala. Her dark, gigantic wings stand out like shadows. Feathers ornament her shimmering greenish dress and head attire. The dark tone of the painting is contrasted by two light objects: a silver trumpet and a white star-formed light on the diadem on her forehead. The painting's message, despite its intensive presence, remains unclear: the tension between the visible and the invisible is driven to a dialectical climax suggesting a 'mystical content'.[8] Like Le Fanu's story, understanding can only be grasped by means of an 'inner sense'. And here, too, access is given by way of Swedenborgian concepts.[9]

The countenance of Watts' angelic being—surrounded by receding, parting clouds—is suggestive of an apocalyptic and thus time-related theme. On the other hand her relaxed mood coupled with the painting's title (which cannot be divorced from it),[10] point towards something permanent and substantial. Both aspects are linked to a view of the human being as eternal and dynamic, in short, the image of a Swedenborgian angel whose final and highest manifestation is to become part of the 'Grand Man'.

From the point of view of the subjective forms related to space and time, the angel and the 'Grand Man' represent the future. The temporal association is found in the receding red clouds of the dawn. Here the human being is pictured in a higher stage of development, of the human soul being freed from its 'cloud' of imprisonment.[11] The reference to eternity appears in the white light of the (morning) star and the distant gaze. According to Swedenborg, 'the angels constantly turn their Faces to the Lord as the Sun'.[12] The 'Sunrise of Eternity' is consequently apocalyptic, representing the end of times and, therefore, the *timeless*.

As with the story of Sheridan Le Fanu, one can see here that it is Swedenborgian theosophy which gives to the metaphysical concern of Symbolism in the late 19th century its images and concepts. In Le Fanu's story of Mr Justice Harbottle, it is the image of Hell; in Watts' painting, that of Heaven.

In what follows, Symbolism is understood as a movement in European art from around 1850 to 1920. But there is also strong evidence that the inward dynamic of Symbolism continues to the present day, especially in cinematic art, its concern being to penetrate the superficial character of phenomena, the veil of the world of appearances. Symbolism emerged alongside, and in contrast to, the realistic and materialistic tendencies of the late 19th century, crossing the borders between the arts (i.e., painting, sculpture, narrative and poetic literature); psychology; the natural sciences; theology; and mythological research. Watts defined it as the 'spiritual yearning' for 'something beyond [. . .] heaven's infinity',[13] and Emily Brontë (whose work carries Symbolist traces) described the interest in something inscrutable and strange when she wrote:

> There cast my anchor of desire
> Deep in unknown eternity
> Nor ever let my Spirit tire
> With looking for *What is to Be*.[14]

The methods of presentation found in Symbolist art rest on an understanding of Existence (or Being) as multi-layered—emerging from somewhere unseen ('the depths') — and in this way it is connected with what is called 'tradition' in philosophy, the notion that there is a deeper meaning under the surface of everyday reality. This meaning may have been visible at the very beginning of human consciousness (*aletheia*), but has since become withdrawn, clouded within mystery. It was precisely the analysis of these depths that was re-invigorated through Swedenborg (as part of Neoplatonic legacy) and, what is equally important, it occurred during an age when interests were increasingly centred upon a concept of lifeless, mechanically reacting nature. Essentially, Swedenborg's world-view is identical with the Symbolists in that human existence is thought to be a mirror of nature, in which figures are inseparably linked within landscape motifs. As such, the referential character of such landscape images—whether natural descriptions, re-presentations of atmospheric and meteorological phenomena, townscapes or dream landscapes—serve to represent symbolically the inner status of these figures, and, on the whole, the general inner status of the developing modern age. All landscapes possess a double meaning in the sense that they contain at the same time both apocalyptic and material characteristics. The emphasis here, however, concerns the apocalyptic.

This apocalyptic character of the symbolic landscapes has to be approached or understood in a specific way. Emerging hand in hand with the rise of the modern world, the theme of the Apocalypse appears from the 14th century onwards expressing a fearful and widespread mood of the 'end of the world'.[15] The outbreak of the plague, the influence of new powerful technologies (such as firearms, instruments of torture and other innovations) and social and commercial change created real fears and a sense of being under siege. 'Ideological' threats also appeared, the consequence of imperialistic attitudes towards the world, and the shadows of beings who were murdered or pushed into a no man's land, returned in the form of mental pictures, such as the 'Antichrist, Satan, witches, evil spirits and the like'.[16]

In addition to this understanding of the Apocalypse—orientated on a one-track view of time—a further and essentially more complex interpretation of the apocalyptic phenomenon also manifested. This second interpretation can be characterized as 'chiliastic' and—under the strong influence of Paracelsus, Jacob Boehme, and not least of Swedenborg—it forms a world-view present in Romantic and Symbolist art and continues to the present day in the work of David Lynch and Jim Jarmusch. In contrast to the one-track view of time (a giving-oneself-up to an unavoidable Apocalypse), this other way of looking (that only becomes possible through a 'vertical' rising above the 'horizontal' stream of time) opens a perspective by which the Apocalypse is *revealed*, e.g. beyond time there opens to the 'inner eye' the great constellations that supersede time, which 'rise over the spirit who beholds'.[17] The apocalyptic aura of the end of time is seen when the human spirit leaves behind his participation in time, 'something more than the sun, greater than the light is coming',[18] as the effect of a movement, or of something 'coming'. The apocalyptic 'impression' becomes in this way strengthened. Through a comprehensive view of the structure of what is real, the immediate dependence of outer objects (the *apparentia*) on spiritual principles (the *entia*) becomes clear. This is one of Swedenborg's central thoughts. With it, the actual real world stands in relationship to the world of appearances by means of 'judgment'.

Though the possibility of experiencing the beyond is no longer something given (of an essential reality perceived through an overwhelming presence of phenomena), it is still present as something divined. But it can no longer fulfil the function of a signpost. As a consequence, in this multiple interlinked labyrinth, the conjunction of *all* possible directions leads one astray. We can see this, for example, in David Lynch's films *Twin Peaks* and *Mulholland Drive*, and it can also be found in the late work of George MacDonald.

In Symbolist art, especially Symbolist landscape art, one can also observe the losing of oneself in the opaqueness of phenomena. Symbolist landscape makes use of a complex scheme of 'indicators' as bearers of messages, a procedure corresponding to the viewpoint of Swedenborg: 'This world itself is not an unconditionally real but a lower "natural" condition of humanity, whose characteristic is precisely that here *apparentia* are regarded as, or fixed as, *entia*'.[19] Consequently, such 'indicators', which are related to transcendent, metaphysical worlds of imagination, stand alone, isolated in a labyrinth, a desert of the factual world without any background, appearing like 'dreams not from this world'.[20] And yet, because these 'indicators' are architecturally structured, they can still be recognized as 'signs'. Signs of this kind can be motifs, symbols, metaphors or colourful epithets. For instance, the colour of white light (which often appears with negative connotations, as in Melville's *Moby Dick*, or with an ambiguous message, as in Whistler's painting *The White Girl*) and the colour blue (representing the hereafter, an 'azure' or metaphysical blue) occupy a central place. Drawing on motifs from Swedenborg, the warm, bright orange-red of the sunrise in Watts' portrait carries with it symbolic significance.[21]

The works of the Scottish poet and novelist George MacDonald, with regard to Symbolism, are but little observed or researched. The orthodox stance, originating from C S Lewis, of viewing the prose works as either mythopoetic or realistic was long accepted as dogma by most critics.[22] Yet an unbiased reader cannot easily overlook the fact that MacDonald is an impressive Symbolist writer. Moreover, his oeuvre is certainly penetrated by a partly implicit, partly explicit relation to Swedenborg's thought-world, and from this aspect might also be seen to stand within the context of Symbolism. The differences between MacDonald's 'realistic' and 'fantastic' works pale into insignificance. His oeuvre can be more clearly recognized as a unified and complete work of art, which throughout is concerned with the central themes of love, death, dreams and the ideal. Symbolist techniques, like parable structures, storytelling methods of indicating and keeping things hidden, and metaphysically-orientated elements of colour, serve as indicators pointing the way out of the labyrinth of daily life. No work of MacDonald foregoes the 'Symbolist mentality' of both being given up to the darkness of the world and a sense of a relationship to the 'dream of the beyond'.

'All visible objects are but pasteboard masks', Captain Ahab remarks in Melville's *Moby Dick*, 'but in each event [...], some unknown but still reasoning thing puts forth the mouldings of its features from behind the unreasoning mask'. This 'double' experience is also manifested in MacDonald's apocalyptic landscapes. There are the exalted mountains coupled by caves and tunnels, and the king's city and palace peopled by mean persons and traitors in *The Princess and Curdie*; there is the strange blue ice-cave and the menacing labyrinthine hazel-walk and the revelation of the sublime through the appearances of the Jungfrau and the Eiger in *Wilfrid Cumbermede*; likewise one will find the crumbling down of the traditional religious painting of the Last Judgment at the beginning of the earthquake in *A Rough Shaking*. Furthermore, *Phantastes, Lilith, The Wise Woman, The Portent, Sir Gibbie,* and *Weighed and Wanting* all contain Symbolist motifs, for example: paranormal happenings, landscapes heavy with meaning, or sudden apocalyptic weather in the shape of strange clouds, storms, floods, and earthquakes.

Not only in the use of the parable structure, which is based on the concept of Correspondences, Swedenborg's philosophy and mysticism is also present in innumerable individual motifs in the complete works: Wilfrid Cumbermede's white horse, for example, is only explained when it is recognized as the judge's horse[23] which is the meaning given by Swedenborg (in *De Equo Albo*) to the bearer of the Word of Love. Love (or loving-kindness) that renounces spiritual violence is the central theme of this novel. Wilfrid is aspiring towards it; his personality is in the process of growing. His uncle, Sir David Cumbermede Darryl, should be understood as the ideal state of such a personality; he is human perfection. Both Wilfrid and his uncle are 'a-sexual' in the sense of 'beyond sexuality'. They represent the integration of man as a whole, perhaps as an angelic 'third gender'.[24] Here again, we see beings who appear to be humans but in reality are angels or on the way to 'angelhood', a motif deeply tinted by Swedenborgian thinking. Even the phenomenon of degenerate man, whose descent can be read more or less obviously from his physiognomy, is found in the novel in the figure of Coningham. Such themes also appear, but less enigmatically, in Lilith's manifestations in *Lilith* and in the animal-people in the king's household in *The Princess and Curdie*.

Swedenborg's teaching of the 'Grand Man' here is of central importance. The 'Grand Man' is the divine life manifested in human form and with it *the* origin and source of the whole universe, as well as the 'form of the future community of the redeemed spirits'.[25] Related to the human being himself, the 'Grand Man' is both the archetype of every single spiritual personality and the archetypal form of the community of all these personalities. This Being, pointing beyond the elements of time—both 'backwards' to our origins and 'forwards' to a goal beyond time—is symbolized by MacDonald in the figure of a child. In a more theoretically based image from *The Golden Key* he is also the oldest of all human beings 'the old Man of the Fire', a naked child at play. In a stronger, more active image, he appears in Diamond and Sir Gibbie. The defencelessness and original uncorrupted goodness of both are revealed, as it is said of Sir Gibbie:

> [...] his heart the one gulf, into which the dead-sea wave rushes with no recoil—from which ever flows back only purest water, sweet and cool; [...] there, in its own cradle, the primal order is still nursed, still restored.[26]

In *Phantastes*, the Divine Human (Blake's Swedenborgian vocabulary) is shown to Anodos's inner eye as the prophecy of a new humanity organized through love. The purified human being—in a new form, 'a winged Child'[27] in 'a floating chariot'[28]—may see in advance what appears impossible to space-time experience:

> knowing [...] that despair dies into infinite hope, and that the seeming impossible there, is the law here! But, O pale-faced woman, and gloomy-browed men, and forgotten children, how I will wait on you, and minister to you, and, putting my arms about you in the dark, think hope unto your hearts, when you fancy no one is near![29]

In the penultimate chapter of *Lilith* the 'Grand Man' is revealed as the 'beautifullest man' firstly before the eyes of children, then through those of the narrator (Vane) as a 'great quivering [...] compact of angel faces',[30] and finally to everyone in the figure of their own Mother and the inexhaustible, fruitful Nature: 'all kind of creatures [...] all in one heavenly flash'.[31] In the ensuing description of Nature as the mystical marriage of heaven and earth, rocks and water, river and the city on the rock, MacDonald shows the apocalyptic Symbolist landscape, which represents the 'Grand Man' as the anticipation of eternity. *Phantastes* on the other hand shows a picture of the end in two separate spheres: an evening sky where feathery clouds drift high above the world reddened by the already descending sun and a large town in the depths out of which cries of hopelessness and despair arise.[32]

Under the effect of Swedenborg's theosophy and mysticism, the accent of the pictorial nature of artistic creations of the late 18th and 19th centuries shifts from an interpretation of the real towards a study of the inner nature of the human being. Even though Kant's concept of knowledge is essentially 'more mechanistic' than those indebted to Swedenborg (e.g. Blake, Coleridge, Schelling and Solov'ev), he too is indebted to Swedenborg for the most essential impulse of the 'relative, subjective character of our space, of time and of the whole mechanical order of appearances which they govern'.[33] During the course of the 19th century, and through the influence of Swedenborg's manner of seeing things, attention becomes concentrated on the dynamic processes that occur in the deepest self. Within the philosophic tradition this is found first in the work of Kierkegaard. It is perhaps no coincidence that in his highly abstract thought (*Fear and Trembling, Repetition, A Crisis in the Life of an*

Actress, and 'Diary of a Seducer' from *Either-Or*) he introduces fictional and narrative structures, or as in *Sickness unto Death* he makes concrete the abstractly produced condition of despair with a suggestive image. (Compare the image of the locked room, the concealed door, the desert, the monastery and the madhouse, in 'The Form of this Sickness (Despair)'. Parallels are also to be found, arising out of similar mental experiences, in Christina Rossetti's 'I lock my door upon myself' and the painting of the same title by Fernand Khnopff, 1891).[34]

Similarly, Symbolist art presents such phenomena and processes with pregnant images of mental landscapes, or else it relates these landscapes (geological formations, towns and places, houses, streets, etc.) directly to the main protagonists of the work. Three examples can show this. In his entire work, Joseph Sheridan Le Fanu aligned himself unmistakeably with the mysticism of Swedenborg. The philosopher and lyric poet Vladimir Solov'ev (1854-1900), the 'father of Russian Symbolism', as a follower of Schelling's thought admired Swedenborg's philosophy. George MacDonald, who carried on a lively dialogue with German romantic philosophy and poetry, but also with the intellectual and artistic streams of his time, met Swedenborg's philosophy and mysticism in the paintings of G F Watts, Rossetti, Millais and Burne-Jones (also indirectly through their meeting French Symbolist painting). MacDonald would also have met it in the work of Blake (whose biography by Gilchrist appeared in 1863), and he directly concerned himself with it—as is most clearly shown by the fashioning and imagery of *Lilith*. In the works of these three writers in particular, their 'own desert places' function as representations of the mental condition of their protagonists, as can be seen, for example, in the role of the 'speaker' in their lyrical poems.

The 'night, which broods within most deeply'[35] is the subject of the *Story of Bartram-Haugh* by Sheridan Le Fanu, whose full, original, title *Maud Ruthyn and Uncle Silas; A Story of Bartram-Haugh* (1864) can also be read as a Victorian sensational novel. This outer impression nevertheless is misleading; the story is concerned with a Swedenborgian parable of hell. Bartram-Haugh a former stately home built from white stone is in decline; its facade is stained and overgrown with moss, the surrounding park and wood have been neglected and become eerie. Eerie, too, is the architectural centre, the inner courtyard of Bartram-Haugh, 'the inner walls of this great house',[36] a courtyard which from a bird's eye-view can be seen framed by a window in the second floor of the house:

[…] a small and dismal quadrangle, formed by the inner walls of this great house, and of course designed only by the architect to afford the needful light and air to portions of the structure. […] The surrounding roof was steep and high. The walls looked soiled and dark. The windows lined with dust and dirt, and the window-stones were in places tufted with moss, and grass, and groundsel. An arched doorway had opened from the house into this darkened square, but it was soiled and dusty; and the damp weeds that overgrew the quadrangle drooped undisturbed against it. It was plain that human footsteps tracked it little, and I gazed into that kind and sinister area with a strange thrill and sinking.[37]

It is not surprising that this 'dreary quadrangle of cut stone'[38] makes such an impression on Maud, the narrator. She knows, though not explicitly, that it has to do with a murder of years past. Does she feel a presentiment that this place is planned as her grave? Both murders, the one accomplished, the other planned, are conceived by her uncle, Silas Ruthyn, in all their refined details. Uncle Silas, who, when viewed superficially, appears as an honourable old man with silver hair, wearing a black, velvet overcoat, is to deeper sight someone 'living dead'. Another character from the novel, the Swedenborgian Dr Bryerly, characterizes him—in sketchy manner from a quotation from Swedenborg's *Heaven and Hell*—as someone damned: 'and it is said, that independently of the physical causes in that state operating to enforce community of habitation, and an isolation from superior spirits, there exist sympathies, aptitudes, and necessities which would, of themselves, induce that depraved gregariousness, and isolation too'.[39] Even for Maud, who initially idolized him, it becomes increasingly clear that he is surrounded by the ghostly aura of a revenant, of one who haunts places from a former life, so that in looking at his unwholesome gaze, she is always reminded of the lines of the Irish poet Thomas Moore (1779-1852):

Oh, ye dead! Oh, ye dead! whom we know by the light you give
From your cold gleaming eyes, though you move like men who live.[40]

His brother Austin Ruthyn of Knowl, Maud's father, appears in the eyes of his daughter always 'like a portrait with a background of shadow [. . .] and then again in silence fading nearly out of view'.[41] Silas produces the effect of 'an apparition drawn as it seemed in black and white'.[42] From their behaviour, the brothers appear as opposites, yet the ghostly colourlessness attributed to them makes them both belong to the undead. The pious, pompous Austin and the seemingly religious, demonic Silas are uprooted existences, symbolically demonstrated by the 'two giant trees, overthrown at last by the recent storm, lying with their upturned roots, and their yellow foliage still flickering on the sprays that were to bloom no more'.[43] Yet the desolate inner courtyard with its dirty stone walls and opaque windows symbolizes in the clearest way Silas's 'died-off individuality' (Kierkegaard) isolated from life. The strangled light, the overgrown gate, the non-existence of 'human footsteps' show the inner courtyard as an inner life that can no longer justify its own existence, as the courtyard can no longer allow 'the needful light and air' to enter the house. The rank growth of grass and weeds in the courtyard and on the architecture points towards an eerie, rank, demonic activity.

The choking, wet, decaying atmosphere offers comparison with Tennyson's 'lonely moated grange', yet the sadly noble, romantic quality is missing. The inner courtyard of Bartram-Haugh manifests a hopeless emptiness and desolate boredom, a place of hell. According to Silas's plan, it is to become Maud's grave. Maud herself almost succumbs to the fateful bann with which this place with the negative energy of a black hole exerts on her.

Although the inner courtyard of Bartram-Haugh is a place of stagnation, it contains apocalyptic themes: the dynamic of suction and a movement into the depths. It is, as we have seen, the depths of the grave. The last thing that the reader experiences of this place is the clanking of a spade digging Maud's grave. The structure of the suction towards this point is already shown during the drive to Bartram, a journey into the valley, 'descending at a great pace' into a thickly wooded, 'narrow valley', and finally with accelerating speed, 'almost a gallop', up to a wall with a fantastic iron gate. Here the actual surroundings of the 'enchanted castle' begins.[44] As the novel demonstrates, the way out of this magic bann, the escape out of this eerie suction, is almost impossible.

Vladimir Solov'ev's poem 'Waking Dream', of January 1895, also takes as its theme the approach to an unknown goal, and which, incidentally, is also situated in a wood. 'The word "wood" does not only suggest a group of trees that can be young or old; a shudder immediately runs down one's back', says the symbolist painter Puvis de Chavannes (1824-98), who uses the motif of a dark impenetrable, threatening, wood in his paintings.[45] Woods are an ancient traditional image, pointing far back in the history of motifs via Blake's 'forests of the night' and Paracelsus' imagination of nature as a wood burning up into smoke[46] and Dante's 'selva oscura'. The Greek word 'hyle', meaning 'matter', originally meant 'wood'. The fairytale imagery of a hero or heroine lost in a wood portrays the soul lost in, or captured by, the realm of matter.

In Solov'ev's poem the wood lying behind the speaker contributes to the diffuse, sinister mood of the work, rendered denser through the heavy clouds, fog and all-embracing desert of snow. Nevertheless, there are two phenomena which burst through the mood. A prose translation of this poem in two verses or stanzas is as follows:

An azure eye / Through dark heavy clouds [...] / Sinking in deeply / Through a desert of loose snow / Towards a mysterious goal / I go alone. / Behind me only pine trees / All around into the widths / Spreads the wide lake in its white garment, / And the stillness speaks loudly to me: the unexpected will soon be fulfilled.

The azure eye / Has sunk again into the fog, / In lonely pain / Hope of meeting again fades. / The sad pine trees / Dark in the distance, motionless, / The desert without goal / The path without striving, / And ever the same voice without reproof sounds out of the stillness: / The end approaches near, the unexpected will soon be fulfilled.[47]

The environment, in which the speaker finds himself in the image of a lonely wanderer, bears all the signs of a 'wilderness', far removed from civilization. 'Orientation' cannot be found, and as such the wilderness becomes a symbol of an exceptional condition, of a 'pre-visionary' state. The wood, the pine trees 'darkening in the distance, motionless', represent the natural, physical world which the speaker has left behind. Now he is surrounded by a white landscape, a snowy desert and a 'wide' lake before him.

The given context makes it clear that this white is not that of the Symbolists, of light in the positive sense, in which 'white bell-flowers' live as 'white thoughts / on the secret paths of thy soul': 'Thou wanderest on thy dark path, / we shine motionless in the stillness'.[48] In the 'Waking Dream', it is the white which we know from Adalbert Stifter's *Bergkristall* ('Mountain Crystal'): white without a signpost. The melancholic atmosphere of dark, heavy clouds, of fog, without visual and aural incentives, produces stillness, the prophetic or holy stillness (a frequent motif in Solov'ev's lyrics). This makes the two impressions perceptible, which are obviously not 'normal' sense impressions, although they manifest as something 'seen' and 'heard'. At the beginning of each verse the visual impression is described, and at the end of the verse the aural one. In the sky the 'azure eye' is opened, as if the speaker, for a moment, could see the blue of the sky through a rent in the clouds. Yet the metaphor at the same time means both 'seeing' and 'being seen', so that one can speak better of an eye-contact, as Solov'ev describes it in his poem 'Meeting' (1898):

> If you forget yourself during the day or if you awake around midnight / somebody is there [...] Straight into the soul gaze the radiant eyes. [...] And like dew in the ocean are dissolved for ages / all the days of life.[49]

The *azure gaze*, through the vocabulary of colour of the beyond—defined as metaphysical phenomenon—has nevertheless only been perceptible for a timeless 'moment'. The tension of 'now/seeing' and 'already/having disappeared' is paralleled in the oxymoron, 'eloquent stillness'. They 'loudly' announce that 'something' comes to an end and the unexpected is fulfilled.

The theme of the poem, then, is an apocalyptic event. At a place which suggests desolation, in a glimpse through a rent in the clouds, a direct contact is produced with the apocalyptic fundamental structure of reality itself. It is as if Swedenborg's Correspondences, which as a rule are of parallel structure (in the case of divination), touch each other and are united.[50] In Solov'ev's poem, Swedenborg's three worlds—natural world (human intelligence), spiritual world (rationality) and divine world (divine wisdom)—are brought together in a 'short circuit' resulting in a vision.

Using the metaphor of the mental landscape, Solov'ev's poem 'Waking Dream' presents an exceptional condition of consciousness, the view of the end of the world. On the other hand, the mental landscape which George MacDonald sketches at the beginning of *Lilith*, presents that of the archetypal human being *before* the beginning of time. It is a soul's view of the material world before it descends, enters and becomes involved in it. In the context of the Neoplatonic tradition, which Swedenborg also represents, Vane's story is that of traversing the world of the soul, which begins with an observation, a short pause before the 'way down' into 'getting involved'[51] and continues with a growing 'involution' into the (material) world and frees itself in a turning-about, or 'return' out of this involution. Through a positive interpretation of this ontological-anthropological pattern, which MacDonald advocates, this return does not signify that the human being leaves the material world behind without changing and enriching it. Rather, through his having descended, the human being leads the world up to a higher level, having enriched it by the very essence of the soul which gives its light away. In his *Timaeus*, Plato compares the soul to an inverted tree which is rooted in heaven and whose branches and twigs grow down to the earth;[52] Plotinus, in turn, stresses that the soul's descent is necessary for the perfection of the whole,[53] whilst Schelling can be compared with Swedenborg when he says:

> God did not want something dead or necessary, but a free and living band of both (the outer and the inner world), and the word of this connection was carried by the human being in his heart and on his lips.[54]

Of course, the world would not be able to be transformed and enriched by the divine light of the human soul unless there was a substantial connection between both.

Should we not be allowed to assume there has been a divine decree, that *this nature is initially raised to the human stage* in order to find in it the connecting point of both worlds, and that afterwards through the human being an immediate transition from the one into the other can occur; what grows in the outer world *can without interruption continue to grow in the inner or the spirit-world?*[55]

According to Swedenborg, in the material and the spiritual world there is nothing which essentially can exist outside the unfolding divine life.[56]

MacDonald's narrator Vane views the mental landscape before all time, which is simultaneously both a picture he observes as something distinct from himself and the mirror in which he sees himself: 'Could I have mistaken for a mirror the glass that protected a wonderful picture?'[57] At the moment the mirror ceases to be a mirror and becomes the picture of a landscape which one enters, in which one 'becomes involved': the timeless moment of hesitation and of observing, is over. The beginning of time and thus, of the story (in *Lilith* of *a* story) begins. The Neoplatonic tradition interprets this moment as 'becoming caught' through seeing your own image in a mirror, a motif cited by Thomas Taylor in the orphic myth of Bacchus.[58]

MacDonald, describing the mental landscape of the archetypal human being, writes:

> I saw before me a wild country, broken and heathy. Desolate hills of no great height, but somehow of strange appearance, occupied the middle distance; along the horizon stretched the tops of a far-off mountain-range; nearest me lay a tract of moorland, flat and melancholy.[59]

The crowded and compact textual passage describes with extreme neutrality the monotonous moorland. No brightening colour words are used; only the most general information is given in the form of the appearances and the positioning of the content in the image. These, for the most part, are the adjectives 'wild', 'heathy', 'strange', 'far-off' and 'flat and melancholy'. They are used to describe the elements of the landscape 'country', 'hills', 'horizon', 'mountain-range', 'moorland', to which the imagination of the reader can orientate itself, and which point beforehand to the heroic plot: 'heroic' because it is about the daring venture to bring divine light into the natural world.

The restriction of linguistic means and the characteristic style of the sentences, which seem to evoke the very landscape formations by sound and grammar, convey to the reader an intensive enticement and a challenge, participating in the narrator's experiences upon observing the picture. It could be best described in Novalis' word *Die Erwartung*. It is 'a wonderful picture', which hieroglyphically symbolizes both the plot of the novel and the meaning of the work.[60]

NOTES

[1] Joseph Sheridan Le Fanu, 'Honourable Mr Justice Harbottle', in *In a Glass Darkly* (Wordsworth Classics, 1995), p. 98.

[2] Ibid., p. 100.

[3] Ibid., p. 75.

[4] Ernst Benz, *Emanuel Swedenborg: Visionary Savant in the Age of Reason,* tr. Nicholas Goodrick-Clarke (West Chester PA: Swedenborg Foundation, 2002), p. 391.

[5] For the concept of mental landscape see Anne Jerslew, *David Lynch. Mentale Landschaften* (Vienna: Passagen, 1976), pp. 19 ff. and 27 ff.

[6] G F Watts, *The Dweller in the Innermost* (1885-6, Tate Britain).

[7] For Swedenborg the left hand is the hand of love and the right the hand of wisdom, cf. Kathleen Raine, *Blake and Tradition* (London: Routledge & Kegan Paul, 1969), vol. I, p. 7.

[8] Armin Knigge, *Die Lyrik Vl. Solov'evs und ihre Nachwirkung bei A Belyj und A Blok* (Amsterdam: Adolf Hakkert, 1973), p. 156.

[9] Watts and his circle of friends had Swedenborgian sympathies. See Andrew Wilton, Barbara Bryant et al, *The Age of Rossetti, Burne-Jones & Watts: Symbolism in Britain 1860-1910* (London: Tate Gallery, 1997).

[10] It took 14 years (from 1866 to 1880) before the painting received its final title.

[11] Cf. Kathleen Raine, *Blake and Tradition*, vol. I, p. 8.

[12] Emanuel Swedenborg, *The Wisdom of Angels concerning Divine Love and Divine Wisdom* (London, 1788), §129 and §120.

[13] M S Watts, *George Frederic Watts* (London: MacMillan and Co, 1912), vol. III, *His Writings*, 'The Aims of Art' (1888), p. 232.

[14] Edward Chitham and Tom Winnifrith (eds.), *Selected Brontë Poems* (Oxford: Blackwell, 1985), p. 169.

[15] Jean Delumeau, *Angst im Abendland. Die Geschichte kollektiver Ängste im Europa des 14. bis 18. Jahrhunderts* [Ger tr. of Fre *Le péché et la peur: la culpabilisation en Occident XIIIe-XVIIIe siècles*], tr. Monika Hübner (Reinbek bei Hamburg: Rowohlt, 1989), vol. II, p. 313 ff.

[16] Karl Georg Zinn, *Kanonen und Pest. Über die Ursprünge der Neuzeit im 14. und 15. Jahrhundert* (Opladen: Westdeutscher Verlag, 1989), p. 15.

[17] Cf. Plotinus, *The Enneads*, V.5.

[18] George MacDonald, *Phantastes and Lilith* (Grand Rapids, MI: Wm. B. Eerdmans, 1976), p. 256.

[19] Vladimir Solov'ev, *Philosophie. Theologie. Mystik* (Baden: Wewel, 1965), ch. 'Emanuel Swedenborg', p. 532.

[20] Solov'ev, 'Noch einmal weisse Glockenblumen' [Once again white daffodils], in Knigge, *Die Lyrik Vl. Solov'evs*, p. 90.

[21] See for example G F Watts, *The Dweller in the Innermost* and *After the Deluge* (c.1885-91).

²² Cf. Adelheid Kegler, 'Der Schlaf der Seele: Die Verschmelzung traditionaler und Swedenborgianischer Denkstrukturen in M.s *Lilith*', in *Inklings Jahrbuch*, 2002, p. 26 ff.; and Kegler, 'Wilfrid Cumbermede: A Novel in the context of European Symbolism', in *North Wind*, no. 21, 2002, p. 71 ff.

²³ The Book of Revelation 19: 11-21.

²⁴ Cf. Peter von Moos, 'Das mittelalterliche Kleid als Identitätssymbol und Identifikationsmittel', in von Moos (ed.), *Unverwechselbarkeit. Persönliche Identität und Identifikation in der vormodernen Gesellschaft* (Cologne: Weimar, Vienna: Böhlau, 1969), p. 396.

²⁵ Benz, *Swedenborg*, p. 378.

²⁶ George MacDonald, *Sir Gibbie* (London: Hurst and Blackett, 1880), p. 123.

²⁷ MacDonald, *Phantastes and Lilith*, p. 165.

²⁸ Ibid., p. 179. Blake comments on Swedenborg's imagination of 'a thin white cloud' as a picture of a spirit, or angel, which ultimately represents a human being, in a marginal note to his copy of Swedenborg's *Divine Love and Wisdom*: 'Think of a white cloud as being holy, you cannot love it; but think of a holy man within the cloud, love springs up in your thoughts [. . .]'. See Raine, *Blake and Tradition*, vol. I, p. 13.

²⁹ MacDonald, *Phantastes and Lilith*, pp. 179-80.

³⁰ An explicit reference to Swedenborg, *Divine Love and Wisdom*, §129 and §120: 'The universal Heaven, which Consisteth of Myriaden of Myriaden of Angels, in its universal Form is as a man; so also is every Society in Heaven, as well great as small'. (Also quoted in Raine, *Blake and Tradition*, vol. I, p. 204.)

³¹ MacDonald, *Phantastes and Lilith*, pp. 416-17.

³² Ibid., p. 179.

³³ Solov'ev, *Philosophie. Theologie. Mystik*, ch. 'Emanuel Swedenborg', p. 532.

³⁴ Fernand Khnopff, *I Lock my Door upon Myself* (1891, Neue Pinakothek, Munich).

³⁵ Søren Kierkegaard, *Die Tagebücher* [The Journals], tr. Theodor Haecker (Munich: Küsel, 1953), in an entry for the year 1843.

³⁶ Joseph Sheridan Le Fanu, *Uncle Silas*, ed. W J McCormack (Oxford & New York: OUP, 1981), p. 213.

³⁷ Ibid., p. 213.

³⁸ Ibid., p. 400.

³⁹ Ibid., p. 232.

⁴⁰ Ibid., p. 256.

⁴¹ Ibid., p. 2.

⁴² Ibid., p. 190.

⁴³ Ibid., pp. 182-3.

⁴⁴ Ibid., p. 182.

⁴⁵ See for example Puvis de Chavannes' *Death and the Maiden* (1872, Sterling and Francine

Clark Art Institute, Williamstown, MA).

[46] Raine, *Blake and Tradition*, vol. II, p. 16.

[47] Translated from the German, in Knigge, *Die Lyrik Vl. Solov'evs*, p. 126.

[48] Ibid., p. 144. Even the white bell-flowers of Solov'ev's first bell-flower poem, in spite of their positive message (they point to the aim of the aspiration), suggest a slightly uncanny connotation arising from the ambiguity that they are white and motionless.

[49] Ibid., p. 30.

[50] Cf. Benz, *Swedenborg*, p. 351.

[51] Cf. MacDonald, *Phantastes and Lilith*, p. 193: 'How did I get here?'

[52] Plato, *Timaeus*, 90AB.

[53] Plotinus, *The Enneads*, IV.8.1.

[54] Schelling, *Sämtliche Werke*, First series (Stuttgart: Cotta, 1862), vol. IX, pp. 37-8.

[55] Ibid.

[56] Cf. Benz, *Swedenborg*, p. 363 ff.

[57] MacDonald, *Phantastes and Lilith*, p. 192.

[58] Thomas Taylor, *A Dissertation on the Eleusinian and Bacchic Mysteries* (Amsterdam, 1790), pp. 135-6 and 147-8.

[59] MacDonald, *Phantastes and Lilith*, p. 192.

[60] Cf. Swedenborg's use of hieroglyph motives in *Arcana Caelestia*, quoted by Benz in *Swedenborg*, p. 354.

Eros and the Unknown Victorian:
Coventry Patmore and Swedenborg

Richard Lines

T he Victorian poet Coventry Patmore (1823-96), once famous (and even notorious in some circles) for his long poem in praise of love and marriage, *The
Angel in the House*, is, sadly, little remembered today, except among some
Catholics, Patmore having been received into the Roman Catholic Church in 1864 two
years after his first wife's death. While his importance as a Catholic poet and writer of
prose is recognized (particularly for his later and more difficult volume of verse, *The
Unknown Eros*, and for his last prose work, *The Rod, the Root and the Flower*), he
deserves wider modern readership, and it is noteworthy that the profound influence that
his reading of Swedenborg had on his thought and his writing has not received recent
acknowledgment.[1] By contrast, earlier scholars did know about Swedenborg's influence
on Patmore, Caroline Spurgeon having gone so far as to say that he is 'the English writer
most saturated with Swedenborg's thought'.[2] While this may be an exaggeration
(Swedenborg's influence on Blake and on Patmore's contemporaries, particularly the
Brownings,[3] being equally important), it does help to redress the balance and show that
his reading of Swedenborg had a powerful effect on his own writing. In his comprehensive
study, *The Mind and Art of Coventry Patmore*,[4] J C Reid, while stressing that many of

the poet's concepts (especially with regard to the nature of the love of God for man) owe more to St Bernard of Clairvaux, St Thomas Aquinas and St Augustine than to the Swedish seer, nevertheless concludes that Patmore may justifiably be regarded as, apart from Blake, 'the most completely Swedenborgian of English poets'.[5] I think that Reid, in making this judgement, tends to neglect the extent to which Patmore's contemporaries (Tennyson and D G Rossetti, for instance, as well as the Brownings) were steeped in Swedenborg, but it is remarkable that Patmore, in expressing Swedenborg's ideas, often does so in the philosopher's own language. It will be argued that the influence of Swedenborg on Patmore's writing was profound and long-lasting, although Patmore was never an uncritical admirer, and that this influence can be seen not only in *The Angel in the House* but in the later works as well.

According to his life-long friend Henry Septimus Sutton,[6] a fellow-poet and later a member of the Swedenborgian New Church and a lay preacher in one of its Manchester congregations, Patmore found a Latin edition of Swedenborg's *Delitiae Sapientiae de Amore Conjugiali* (usually known in English as *Conjugial Love*) during his employment as a librarian at the British Museum and 'studied it delightedly and profoundly'.[7] Patmore, through the influence of his friend Richard Monckton Milnes, man of letters and a Member of Parliament, was appointed as one of two 'additional Supernumerary Assistants in the Department of Printed Books' at the Museum in November 1846.[8] Already a published poet, the salary from this post enabled him to marry in 1847 Emily Augusta Andrews, daughter of the Revd Edward Andrews, a Congregational preacher who had been a childhood tutor of John Ruskin. It was Emily who inspired him to write the poem which established his reputation and it was she who was the real 'Angel in the House'. When a popular edition of the poem was issued many years after Emily's death, Patmore dedicated it 'to the memory of her by whom and for whom I became a poet'.[9] Patmore may have been influenced to read Swedenborg by Ralph Waldo Emerson who visited England in 1847/8 and lectured on Swedenborg as one of history's 'representative men'.[10] Patmore was introduced to Emerson by Henry Sutton and invited him to his house in Camden Town where he introduced him in turn to Alfred Tennyson. Yet Patmore, often critical of Emerson, particularly of his attitude to religion, never referred to him in connection with Swedenborg. He uses Coleridge's description of the Swedish thinker as 'the man of ten centuries' several times and it may have been his reading of Coleridge (rather than Emerson) which brought him to Swedenborg.[11]

The Angel in the House, the first part of which was published in 1854 and the second in 1856, is set as a series of twelve 'Cantos' interspersed by short pieces on the subject of love between men and women. It tells the story of Felix Vaughan, a Cambridge graduate who woos and eventually wins the hand of Honoria Churchill, daughter of the Dean of Sarum (i.e. Salisbury).[12] The prologue tells how Vaughan, while walking with his wife and their children through the fields on their eighth wedding anniversary, tells her of the poem he plans:

> Then she: 'What is it, Dear? The Life
> 'Of Arthur, or Jerusalem's Fall?'
> 'Neither: your gentle self, my Wife,
> 'And love, that grows from one to all.' [13]

The Angel in the House is a much misunderstood poem. Some contemporaries derided it as a celebration of dull domesticity. Edmund Gosse wrote that Patmore was 'this laureate of the tea-table, with his humdrum stories of girls that smell of bread and butter'.[14] In so far as it is known at all today the poem is regarded as celebrating an outdated notion of marriage and womanhood. While it is true that the poem contains a wealth of necessarily contemporary domestic detail, it does reflect Patmore's profound belief in the spiritual nature of the nuptial bond. Married love was, as Reid puts it, 'the only kind which completes the identity of the "homo", that satisfaction of personality which each sex seeks in the other'.[15] Swedenborg taught that the heart of true marriage was the union of love and wisdom, those 'qualities' that constitute the nature of the divine. The woman *represents* love and the man wisdom. In an early essay that appears to reflect his reading of Swedenborg's *Conjugial Love,* Patmore wrote: 'The *affections* of the woman are developed beyond those of the man, pretty nearly to the same extent that the understanding of the man is developed beyond that of the woman'.[16]

He expresses this poetically in *The Angel*:

Were she but half of what she is,
He twice himself, mere love alone,
Her special crown, as truth is his,
Gives title to the worthier throne;
For love is substance, truth the form;
Truth without love were less than nought; [17]

Swedenborg's concept of 'use' is also reflected in the poem:

Can ought compared with wedlock be
For use? But He who made the heart
To use proportions joy. What He
Has join'd let no man put apart. [18]

In *Heaven and Hell* Swedenborg wrote of 'the conjugial delight', which is 'a purer and more exquisite delight of touch' and which 'transcends all the rest because of its use, which is the procreation of the human race and thereby of angels of heaven'. [19] Patmore, like Swedenborg, showed no Jansenist or Manichaean contempt for the physical aspects of married love. [20]

How long shall men deny the flower
Because its roots are in the earth,
And crave with tears from God the dower
They have, and have despised as dearth, [21]

Like Swedenborg also, [22] he emphasizes the 'chastity' of married love with an enthusiasm that shocked some of his Catholic friends, including Aubrey de Vere and Gerard Manley Hopkins. 'Purity', he was to write later, 'ends by finding a goddess where impurity concludes by confessing carrion'. [23]

In 'Deliciae Sapientiae de Amore' (the title of the poem, which translates as 'The Delights of Wisdom concerning Love', is taken directly from Swedenborg's Latin title of

Conjugial Love) from *The Unknown Eros*, [24] Patmore writes of the 'Young Lover true, and love-foreboding maid, / And wedded Spouse, if virginal of thought'. Ahead of his time, Patmore emphasizes the 'unitive' as well as the 'procreative' function of married love. 'The best use of the supremely useful intercourse of man and woman is not the begetting of children, but the increase of contrasted personal consciousness'.[25]

And, though true marriage purpose keeps
Of offspring, as the centre sleeps
Within the wheel, transmitting thence
Fury to the circumference,
Love's self the noblest offspring is,
And sanction of the nuptial bliss. [26]

The Victories of Love, a sequel to *The Angel in the House*, was written during Emily's illness and published just after her death in 1862. Her illness had made him ponder the possibility of the reunion of wedded souls after death, but he had already written in Swedenborgian terms of his faith that marriage love could survive death in *The Angel*:

My faith is fast
That all the loveliness I sing
Is made to bear the mortal blast,
And blossom in a better Spring.
Doubts of eternity ne'er cross
The Lover's mind, divinely clear:
For ever is the gain or loss
Which maddens him with hope or fear: [27]

Swedenborg's teaching, as set out in *Conjugial Love*, is that men and women who have enjoyed a truly spiritual marriage union remain married partners in the next world, but that if the marriage on earth was not an 'inward union', or union of souls, the couple will separate.[28] But what of remarriage in this world after one partner has died? During her fatal illness Emily had written a will in which she bequeathed her wedding-ring to his 'second wife':

> If in a year or two you are able to marry again, do so happily, feeling that if my spirit can watch you, it will love her who makes you happy, and not envy her the reward of a part of your love, the best years of which I have had.[29]

Patmore expresses this thought poetically in *The Victories of Love* in a letter the dying wife Jane writes to her husband Frederick:

> The only bond I hold you to
> Is that which nothing can undo.
> A man is not a young man twice;
> And if, of his young years, he lies
> A faithful score in one wife's breast,
> She need not mind who has the rest.
> In this do what you will dear Love,
> And feel quite sure that I approve.
> And should it chance as it may be,
> Give her my wedding-ring from me;
> And never dream that you can err
> T'wards me by being good to her;

Robert Browning had written similarly of a dying wife's plea to her husband in 'Any Wife to Any Husband' in the volume *Men and Women* published in 1855, but in that poem the wife, although realizing that her husband will seek 'fresher faces' after her death, believes that 'thou must come/Back to the heart's place here I keep for thee'.[30] It is likely that Patmore knew that poem and also Elizabeth Barrett Browning's monumental 'novel in verse', *Aurora Leigh* (1856), the major theme of which is married love and which was also inspired by her reading of Swedenborg.

After Emily's death Patmore visited Rome with his friend the Catholic poet Aubrey de Vere and was later received into the Roman Catholic Church. Not long afterwards he married Marianne Caroline Byles, another Catholic convert, and she became a loving and beloved step-mother to his six children. There seems no doubt that he loved her dearly, although for some years before her death in 1880 she was a chronic invalid. J C Reid suggests that 'the suspension of marital relations' imposed by Marianne's invalidism may have influenced the writing of the 'Psyche' odes in *The Unknown Eros*, as Patmore strove to sublimate his sensual feelings in the spiritual, but he concludes that their marriage was not celibate from the start.[31] In 1881 Patmore married Harriet Robson, his children's governess and a slightly older school-fellow of his daughter, Emily Honoria, who had become a nun in 1875. Harriet bore her husband a son, something which gave him great joy, and, according to J C Reid, his letters to her are 'among the most intimate which have been preserved, and show no diminution in his genius for married love'.[32] Harriet, however, while a loving wife, lacked the intellectual stature of both Emily and Marianne and in his later years Patmore sought solace in his friendship with a younger married woman, the poet and fellow-Catholic, Alice Meynell (1847-1922). Their relationship, although probably never physical, was an intense one. It was tiresome for Harriet and in the end proved too much for Alice Meynell, who turned to the novelist and poet George Meredith as her chief literary mentor. Patmore described his inner struggle to his friend the poet Francis Thompson, who had been rescued from opium addiction by Alice Meynell and her husband Wilfred:

Dieu et Ma Dame [an essay in Patmore's *Religio Poetae*], is the legend of us both. But at present Ma Dame is too much for the balance, peace and purity of my religion. There is too much heartache in it.[33]

Despite his new faith and his love for Marianne and then Harriet, Patmore wrote some of his best poetry in the odes he composed in Emily's memory. 'Departure' (from *The Unknown Eros*) is both poignant, and exquisite in its economy of expression:

It was not like your great and gracious ways!
Do you, that have nought other to lament,
Never, my Love, repent

Of how, that July afternoon,

You went,

With sudden unintelligible phrase,

And frighten'd eye,

Upon your journey of so many days,

Without a single kiss or a good-bye?

But it is in 'A Farewell' (from the same volume) that the Swedenborgian concept of reunion in heaven reasserts itself:

With all my will, but much against my heart,

We two now part.

My very Dear,

Our solace is, the sad road lies clear,

It needs no art,

With faint, averted feet

And many a fear,

In our opposèd paths to persevere.

Go thou to East, I West.

We will not say

There's any hope, it is so far away.

But, O, my Best,

When the one darling of our widowhead,

The nursling Grief,

Is dead,

And no dews blur our eyes

To see the peach-bloom come in evening skies,

Perchance we may,

Where now this night is day,

And even through faith of still averted feet,

Making full circle of our banishment,

Amazèd meet;

The bitter journey to the bourne so sweet

Seasoning the termless feast of our content

With tears of recognition never dry.

In an article published in *The Tablet* in 1978, 'Coventry Patmore and Vatican II', Felicitas Corrigan describes Patmore as the 'poetic genius' of the Second Vatican Council's *Gaudium et Spes* ('Joy and Hope') (1965) and remarks, in the context of a quotation from *The Angel in the House*:

> But human love, however perfect, must come to an end. A startling phrase from *Gaudium et Spes* pulls one up short: 'Widowhood, accepted as a *continuation* of the marriage bond, should be esteemed by all'.[34]

Immediately below this passage she quotes from 'A Farewell' and remarks that the poet 'has constantly hinted at a divine discontent, for human love is but a parable and can never fully satisfy'. I wonder if Patmore would have answered this in Swedenborgian language, saying that the truly conjugial love of man and woman is a perfect mirroring of the divine?

There is no doubt about the sincerity and depth of Patmore's Catholic faith (and that of his second and third wives) and his intense Catholic spirituality is reflected in *The Unknown Eros* and the later prose works, but it should be emphasized that he continued to read Swedenborg and the influence of the Swedish seer remained with him and left its mark. As late as 1891 in a letter to the homoeopathic doctor and translator of Swedenborg James John Garth Wilkinson, Patmore wrote, 'It was Swedenborg mainly that brought me into the Catholic Church'.[35] In the following year, in thanking Wilkinson for the gift of a book, Patmore wrote:

> The 'Summa' of St. Thomas Aquinas and your volume of selections from Swedenborg have, for many years, formed the *groundwork* of all my reading: and you will perhaps be surprised to hear that they seem to me to be but two aspects of one and

the same Catholic truth, St. Thomas appealing mainly to the ear of rational faith, Swedenborg to the perceptive faculty.[36]

Patmore had reviewed Wilkinson's biography of Swedenborg (1849) in the *National Review* in 1858 and it has been noted[37] that Patmore quotes Wilkinson's words describing Swedenborg's imperturbable nature in the closing lines of his poem 'Winter' (from *The Unknown Eros*):

The sphere
Of ether, moved by ether only, or
By something still more tranquil.

Henry Sutton has also attested to Patmore's continuing interest in Swedenborg in later life. He described a visit Patmore made to his house in Manchester in 1883 when, seeing the book shelves loaded with Swedenborg's works, he declared that he was 'my favourite saint'.[38]

Patmore's reading of Swedenborg extended well beyond *Conjugial Love* and its teaching about love and marriage. He also owned copies of the immense *Arcana Caelestia* (which runs to twelve large volumes in the English translation) and *The True Christian Religion*. These books, together with the two volume Index to *Arcana Caelestia*,[39] are, with Patmore's annotations, preserved in the Francis Thompson Room in the Library of Boston College in the United States. J C Reid has a useful Appendix on Patmore's annotations of Swedenborg.[40] While Patmore did not, apparently, read the whole of the *Arcana* (some of the later volumes are uncut), he did make many notes on both volumes of the Index. He was particularly impressed with Swedenborg's exposition of the Doctrine of Correspondences. He wrote, alongside Swedenborg's statement (quoted at page 98 of volume I) that the Science of Correspondences, though now antiquated and lost, far excels all other sciences, 'Poetry is the modern representative of this science', and, in a note at page 855 of volume II, 'It would be worth while to try Swedenborg's system of correspondences in the interpretation of Egyptian hieroglyphics'.[41] Reid asserts that Patmore's essay, 'The Precursor', is 'a thoroughly Swedenborgian interpretation of the significance of St. John the Baptist, the precursor of Christ, as symbolizing the natural love which prepares the way for Divine love'.[42] Like Coleridge before him, Patmore planned (but did not execute) a commentary on Swedenborg's philosophy. He wrote a note on the title page of *The True Christian Religion*: 'Mem: Make epitome of the truths in S's writings, but not in S's language. A most useful book'.[43]

While Patmore was quick to recognize what he considered to be Roman Catholic teaching in Swedenborg, he was critical where he considered him to be in error. He thought that Swedenborg, in his exposition of the Trinity, confused 'Person' with 'Being' and wrote on page 676 of volume II (1860) of the *Arcana* Index:

> Swedenborg's ignorance of the Trinity makes all his account of marriage obscure and dead instead of living and clear to the spirit. Marriage between Persons is a reality; between 'Good' and 'Truth' nothing.[44]

But he wrote that Swedenborg's teaching about the 'proprium' was 'a profound and thorough exposition of the Christian doctrine of "nature" and "grace"'.[45] He thought that Swedenborg's teaching that the Christian church would be one if all Christians had charity, notwithstanding differences of worship and doctrine, was 'pure R. Catholic teaching'.[46]

Patmore did not believe that Swedenborg had been given a special divine mission to lead men and women to the truth and he certainly did not believe that Swedenborg intended to found a new Christian denomination. But he held Swedenborg in high esteem to the end of his life, regarding him, above all, as a great psychologist:

> We have had only one psychologist and human physiologist—at least, only one who has published his knowledge—for at least a thousand years, namely Swedenborg.[47]

It is widely accepted today that Swedenborg's vision of a 'new church' was not of a separate religious denomination, but of a new spirit that would revivify Christianity. Patmore seems to have accepted this and in his essay 'Religio Poetae' wrote of a 'New Dispensation', 'the Dispensation of the Holy Spirit, the Spirit of Life and perceived Reality, continuing and fulfilling the Dispensation of Christ, as His did that of the Father'.[48] Patmore was a faithful son of his own church and a man of his own age holding conservative, and indeed Conservative, views.[49] He did not foresee modern ecumenism, but he did say that he believed in Christianity 'as it will be ten thousand years hence'.[50] Swedenborg's thought left a profound impression on Coventry Patmore and 'he never really cast the Swedish philosopher from his consciousness'.[51]

NOTES

[1] A centenary article by Kenneth Baxter in *The Tablet* (April 23, 1996), 'Victorian values of a thrice-married poet', makes no mention of Swedenborg and, at the time of writing it, the writer had no knowledge of this important connection: letter from Kenneth Baxter to the author.

[2] Caroline Spurgeon, *Mysticism in English Literature* (Cambridge: CUP, 1913), pp. 31-2.

[3] For Swedenborg's influence on the poetry of the Brownings, see my 'Swedenborgian ideas in the poetry of Elizabeth Barrett Browning and Robert Browning', in *In Search of the Absolute*, ed. Stephen McNeilly (London: The Swedenborg Society, 2004), pp. 23-43.

[4] J C Reid, *The Mind and Art of Coventry Patmore* (London: Routledge & Kegan Paul, 1957).

[5] Reid, p. 81.

[6] For Henry Septimus Sutton, see my 'Henry Sutton: Poet, Journalist and New Church Man', in *Annual Journal of the New Church Historical Society for the year 2003* (Chester, 2003), pp. 40-7.

[7] H S Sutton, 'Swedenborg and Coventry Patmore', in *The New-Church Magazine* (London: James Speirs, 1901), p. 179.

[8] Ian Anstruther, *Coventry Patmore's Angel* (London: Haggerston Press, 1992), p. 48.

[9] Coventry Patmore, *The Angel in the House* (London: Cassell, 1887).

[10] Emerson's *Representative Men* was first published in 1850. His essay 'Swedenborg, or the Mystic' has recently been reissued by the Swedenborg Society with an introduction, glossary of names and critical notes as *introducing the Mystic: Emerson on Swedenborg*, ed. Stephen McNeilly (London: The Swedenborg Society, 2003). Emerson did not share Patmore's enthusiasm for *Conjugial Love*: see *introducing the Mystic*, pp. 37-9.

[11] Reid, pp. 46-50. For Coleridge on Swedenborg, see H J Jackson, 'Swedenborg's *Meaning* is the truth: Coleridge, Tulk and Swedenborg', in *In Search of the Absolute*, pp. 1-13.

[12] G F Watts appears to have made an ironic reference to Patmore's poem in the title of his portrait of Lillie Langtry exhibited in 1880, *The Dean's Daughter*. Lillie Langtry, née Emilie Le Breton, *was* a dean's daughter, her father being the Dean of Jersey. When Watts painted her (demurely dressed in black), her affair with the Prince of Wales was already public knowledge.

The connection with *The Angel in the House* would not have been lost on visitors to the Royal Academy when the painting was first exhibited. No mention of this, however, is made in Barbara Bryant's catalogue note for the 2004 exhibition of Watts's portraits at the National Portrait Gallery, London: Barbara Bryant, *G F Watts Portraits: Fame & Beauty in Victorian Society* (London: National Portrait Gallery, 2004), p. 162.

[13] *The Angel in the House*, book I, The Prologue, 4.

[14] Gosse, 'Poems by Coventry Patmore', in *The Athenaeum*, no. 3059, June 12, 1886, p. 771.

[15] Reid, p. 148. Swedenborg's concept of heavenly society as a 'Maximus Homo' or 'Grand Man' comprises, of course, both male and female.

[16] Patmore, 'German Lady Novelists', in *North British Review*, vol. VII, no. XIV, Aug. 1847, p. 371. In *Conjugial Love*, tr. John Chadwick (London: The Swedenborg Society, 1996), §33, Swedenborg wrote that 'the male is by birth a creature of the intellect, the female a creature of the will, or to put the same thing another way, the male acquires from birth an affection for knowing, understanding and being wise, and the female acquires from birth a love of joining herself with that affection in the male'.

[17] *The Angel in the House*, book I, canto v, I. Cf. Swedenborg, *Divine Love and Wisdom*, tr. Clifford and Doris Harley (London: The Swedenborg Society, 1987), §40, where he states that 'love and wisdom are the real and actual substance and form which constitute the subject itself'.

[18] *The Angel in the House*, book II, canto vii, Preludes, I; Cf. Matt.19:6.

[19] Swedenborg, *Heaven and its Wonders and Hell*, tr. Revd J C Ager, rev. Doris Harley (London: The Swedenborg Society, 1992), §402.

[20] Reid, p. 81.

[21] *The Angel in the House*, book I, canto vii, Preludes, II.

[22] Swedenborg, *Conjugial Love*, §143: 'Truly conjugial love is the height of chastity'.

[23] Patmore, 'Imagination', in *Religio Poetae* (London: George Bell & Sons, 1893), p. 107. Patmore's Swedenborgian friend the homoeopathic doctor James John Garth Wilkinson took a similar view. Writing to Henry James Senior in 1850 about the translation he had undertaken of Swedenborg's scientific work *The Generative Organs*, he expressed the view that 'things before invisible and unutterable will be seen to be as clean as the flowers of the field or as the pleasant butterflies, which are the flowers of flowers': quoted in Clement James Wilkinson, *James John Garth Wilkinson* (London: Kegan Paul, Trench, Trübner & Co., 1911), p. 204.

[24] Patmore, *The Unknown Eros* (London: George Bell, 1878).

[25] Patmore, 'Distinction', in *Principle in Art* (London: George Bell & Sons, 1889), p. 63.

[26] Patmore, 'Wedding Sermon' from *The Victories of Love,* (London: Macmillan & Co., 1863).

[27] *The Angel in the House*, book I, canto vii, Preludes, I.

[28] *Conjugial Love*, §49.

[29] Basil Champneys, *Memoirs and Correspondence of Coventry Patmore* (London: George Bell & Sons, 1900), vol. I, p. 133.

[30] Robert Browning's 'By the Fireside' and 'One Word More', both also in *Men and Women*, celebrate married love.

[31] Reid, pp. 27-8. Patmore was much influenced in the writing of *The Unknown Eros* by his reading (in translation) of the sixteenth-century Spanish poet and mystic Juan de la Cruz. The Swedenborgian Arthur Beilby found the erotic mysticism of some of the poems in *The Unknown Eros* hard to take. 'Sponsa Dei' and 'Eros and Psyche', in particular, he thought 'of doubtful taste, trespassing riskily on the border-ground of the forbidden. The effect is a little sickly, like an over-perfumed apartment': 'An Appreciation of Coventry Patmore', in *The New-Church Magazine* (London: James Speirs, 1901), pp. 222, 226.

[32] Reid, p. 28.

[33] Quoted by Derek Patmore, *The Life and Times of Coventry Patmore* (London: Constable, 1949), p. 235 and see Reid, pp. 29-32. At a similar age Robert Browning was deeply attracted to a younger married American woman, Katharine Bronson (albeit that she was separated from her husband): see Pamela Neville-Sington, *Robert Browning: A Life After Death* (London: Weidenfeld and Nicholson, 2004), pp. 230-5.

[34] This article was reprinted in *Second Spring: An International Journal of Faith and Culture*, no.3 (Oxford, 2002), pp. 50-5.

[35] Quoted in Wilkinson, p. 207.

[36] Ibid, p. 208.

[37] Reid, p. 67.

[38] H S Sutton, 'Swedenborg and Coventry Patmore', p. 179.

[39] The Swedenborg Society published the *Arcana* Index in two volumes, the first (running from A to L) in 1853 and the second (running from M to Z) in 1860. A later edition with A to M in volume I and N to Z in volume II was published by the Society in 1865. It appears that Patmore used both the 1860 volumes and volume I at least of the 1865 edition.

[40] Reid, pp. 327-9.

[41] Ibid, p. 72.

[42] Ibid, p. 72. 'The Precursor' is an essay in *Religio Poetae*.

[43] Ibid, p. 329. For Coleridge's proposed commentary on Swedenborg, see Jackson, in *In Search of the Absolute*, p. 4. Patmore wanted the form of his own work to be much like that of Coleridge's *Aids to Reflection*.

[44] Ibid, pp. 328-9. Patmore was commenting on the entry in the 1860 volume relating to 'Marriage'.

[45] Ibid, p. 328. Patmore's annotation, which is on page 935 of volume II of the Index, is dated April 1863.

[46] Ibid, p. 328. The note is on page 133 of volume I of the Index. The edition here is the 1865 one and Patmore was commenting on the entry on 'Doctrine'. In *Arcana Caelestia*, §1799, after referring to the different doctrines of Roman Catholics, Lutherans, Calvinists etc., Swedenborg says that the church would become one if Christians were to make love to the Lord

and charity to the neighbour the chief thing of faith. Doctrinal differences would become no more than shades of opinion which true Christians would leave to individual conscience.

[47] Patmore, 'Knowledge and Science', in *The Rod, the Root and the Flower*, XXXVI (London: George Bell & Sons, 1895), p. 99.

[48] Patmore, 'Religio Poetae', in *Religio Poetae*, p. 8. Reid describes this passage as 'unmistakably Swedenborgian in sentiment', p. 74.

[49] Reid, p. 26, says that his second wife Marianne 'shared her husband's political convictions, and took a prominent part in local Conservative politics'. Marianne's money had enabled him to retire from the British Museum and buy an estate in Sussex.

[50] Champneys, vol. II, p. 29.

[51] Reid, p. 75.

Space: the Final Frontier
O V de Lubicz Milosz and Swedenborg

Gary Lachman

When the Polish surname Milosz is mentioned in connection with the Scandinavian sage Emanuel Swedenborg, the Milosz in question is usually the late Czeslaw Milosz, winner of the Nobel Prize for Literature. Poet, teacher and author of such esteemed works as *The Captive Mind* and *The Land of Ulro*——a work, incidentally, in which Swedenborg figures largely——Czeslaw Milosz has made no secret of the influence Swedenborg has had on his life and work. A good example of his appreciation of Swedenborg can be found in his essay 'Dostoevsky and Swedenborg', collected in *Testimony to the Invisible*, an anthology of essays on Swedenborg which includes contributions by other literary high-flyers, like Jorge Luis Borges, Kathleen Raine, Colin Wilson, and D T Suzuki, to name a few.

Yet there is another Milosz, one less well-known than his younger namesake, who was not only greatly influenced by Swedenborg's life and thought but, if we can be allowed a certain poetic and spiritual license, was also a kind of contemporary of the great religious thinker. And if Czeslaw Milosz has been to some degree a champion of Swedenborg's importance, he has also been a perhaps even more outspoken advocate of the significance of his older namesake's work.

The other Milosz, the one I wish to speak about here, is the Lithuanian poet, novelist and mystic, Oscar Vladislas de Lubicz Milosz (1877-1939), a name, I suspect, that is not too often recognized, even among people who should know more about him.[1] And this group, I believe, includes the readers of Swedenborg. What I hope to do in this essay is make O V de L Milosz a bit more accessible to the people who should know about him, and also to point out some of the areas in which his work bears comparison with that of Swedenborg's. A full explication of all the ways in which Oscar Milosz's ideas coincide, parallel, or contrast with those of Swedenborg's would, unfortunately, require much more space and time than I am able to devote to them here. And in a certain sense, this limitation is apt, as space and time are the central concerns of Milosz's late, mystical writings, *Ars Magna* (1924) and *The Arcana* (1927), the two works we will consider here.

I've said that Oscar Milosz was Lithuanian, but as Czeslaw Milsoz has pointed out, his relative had an equal claim to being Polish; to make matters more complicated, during World War I, Oscar Milosz served in the diplomatic corps of the Russian army. In fact, as Czeslaw Milosz remarks, 'Everything related to his origin and his national options conspires to turn any sketch into the indefiniteness of legend'.[2] O Milosz came of mixed stock: his father was Polish-Lithuanian, his paternal grandmother Italian, his mother Jewish, and he himself chose to live in France and to write in French. He was also fluent in a number of other languages, including English, German and, in later life, Hebrew, which allowed him to read the Bible in the original. As Christopher Bamford, one of Milosz's translators, comments, he was 'that almost impossible creature […] a fully realized Occidental, a true son and heir of the West'.[3] This 'Europeanness' about Milosz is in keeping with his own spiritual connection to the Europe of the late 18th century; he was, in many ways, a child of the Enlightenment, a time when among men of learning and insight, national borders gave way to shared beliefs and values, expressed in an esoteric form in the rise of Freemasonry and other 'mystical' societies. (In later years, Milosz himself wrote extensively about the possibility of a 'united Europe'.) Swedenborg too was a man of this time, and it was among Swedenborg's younger contemporaries that O Milosz felt most spiritually at home. 'By his "elective affinities",' Czeslaw Milosz writes, O Milosz was 'a man of the end of the Eighteenth Century […] We can imagine him as an acquaintance of Cagliostro, as a member of one of the "mystical lodges" or as one of the characters in Goethe's *Wilhelm Meister* […] he would have assigned a higher rank to "the Anonymous Philosopher", Claude de Saint-Martin, than to Kant [...] he was a spiritual brother of those who a hundred years before him had looked for a way out of the trap constructed by a presumptuous Reason'.[4] And one of those who had done much to escape this trap was, of course, Emanuel Swedenborg.[5]

Again, this Enlightenment sensibility, in both an historical and, as we shall see, a mystical sense, provided O Milosz with another means whereby we can detect a similarity to Swedenborg. Milosz's facility with language predestined him, one can believe, for his career as a poet and translator; his translations of Coleridge, Byron, Goethe, Hölderlin, Pushkin and others are highly regarded. But it also provided him with a career in diplomacy. From the end of World War I to the late 1930s, when he retired, Milosz served as a diplomat, working to secure the interests of his chosen nationality, Lithuania. He was a member of the Lithuanian delegation to the Peace Conference of 1919; he was then the Lithuanian Representative to the French government. Between 1920 and 1925, as Chargé d'Affaires, he organized the Legations of Lithuania in Paris and Brussels. In Geneva he was the Lithuanian delegate to the League of Nations. Along with his diplomatic work, O Milosz wrote extensively on political, social and economic issues for a number of journals, all the while continuing with his own creative writing, producing a number of exquisitely beautiful poems in French, as well as the two 'metaphysical' poems we shall discuss shortly, *Ars Magna* and *The Arcana*.

I mention Milosz's diplomatic career because it shows that, like Swedenborg, Milosz was an eminently practical man, able to fulfil demanding duties that would exhaust the capabilities of many, while at the same time carrying on with his own poetic and spiritual pursuits. (Along these lines, one thinks of other poetic yet practical individuals, like Goethe, Novalis, and E T A Hoffmann.[6]) Although, as some have remarked, there was a touch of the quixotic in O Milosz's personality, he was in no way a world-denier nor ineffectual dreamer. As Swedenborg devoted his energies to the practical tasks of an Assessor Extraordinary of Sweden's mining industry, Milosz too performed his duties as a diplomat and statesman with alacrity and panache. This was unusual for a man who was a product of the late-Symbolist sensibilities of the decadent *fin de siècle*, and who at one point advised a close friend that 'the important thing is to live as little as possible in what is called the world of reality'.[7]

Along with these personal similarities, there are also the numerous references to Swedenborg in Milosz's work. Most are positive, some critical, but all are respectful. In fact, it is a characteristic of Milosz's lapidary but very readable style—brought to an elegant English through Czeslaw Milosz's translations—that, even in disagreement (sometimes vehement) with other thinkers he is never less than infinitely tactful and courteous; one invariably has the impression of being addressed by a gentleman of unmistakable aristocratic bearing whose eloquence nevertheless speaks of a profound humility and warmth.[8] Having discovered O Milosz only relatively recently, he has become, for me at least, one of those writers whose voice one comes to appreciate and enjoy as one does a friend's, the kind of writer one spends time with, rather than merely reads.

The following is a sample, by no means exhaustive, of the many references O Milosz makes to Swedenborg in his work. The first chapter of Milosz's metaphysical poem, *Ars Magna*, for example, is entitled 'Epistle to Storge', and by itself it contains quite a few references. *Storge* is an unusual word; here it is used as the name of an allegorical androgynous person; in the original Greek it means love, specifically the love of parents for their children. Readers of Swedenborg will remember the use Swedenborg makes of it in his book *Conjugial Love*. Here Swedenborg writes 'There are indications which show clearly that conjugial love and the love of infants, which is called *storge*, are conjoined'. Later in the same chapter, Milosz writes that 'In *Conjugial Love and Its Pure Delights*, *Divine Love and Wisdom*, *The True Christian Religion* and *The Apocalypse Revealed*, the father of modern science […] indulges in remembering the terrors he experienced in his youth when he considered the creation of space and time'.[9] The question of space and time, as I mentioned, will occupy us a bit further on; here Milosz relates his own reflections on these primary human experiences to those of his esteemed predecessor, whom he honours with the title 'father of modern science', paying homage both to Swedenborg's mystical insights, and to his work as a scientist. Further on in 'Epistle to Storge', Milosz gives us in some detail his understanding of the meaning of love, which for him, as for Swedenborg, is the fundamental reality of existence. 'For me', he writes, 'love always means the eternal feminine divine of Alighieri and Goethe, angelic sentiment and sexuality, virginal maternity, wherein are blended as in a fiery crucible, the adramandonic of Swedenborg, the hesperic of Hölderlin, and the elysian of Schiller'. The 'adramandonic of Swedenborg' refers to 'adramandoni', a rare term, even for Swedenborg, used only once in *Conjugial Love* (§183), in one of the 'Memorable Relations'. Here Swedenborg relates how, during a vision, he came upon a garden in a grove, linked by a bridge with gates on either side. Asking the guardian of the bridge the name of the garden, Swedenborg was told '"Adramandoni", which means the delight of conjugial love'. [10] The term must have struck home with Milosz; in 1918, with the help of the socialite Natalie Clifford Barney, he published a collection of poems entitled *Adramandoni*.

Angelic sexuality is one of the central themes of Swedenborg's writings on heaven. For both Milosz and Swedenborg, the love between a man and a woman is symbolic of the relationship between the Creator and Creation; for both the Arcanum of marriage goes to the very heart of being. The *conjunctio oppositorum* is the metaphysical 'glue' that keeps the universe together. This anthropomorphic ontology is linked to an even greater sin—at least according to orthodox cosmologists—committed by Swedenborg, Milosz, and many other mystical thinkers, like the poet William Blake (a serious reader of Swedenborg) and the ancient Kabbalists and Hermetic sages: the idea that the universe itself is a Great Man, or Universal Human. Heaven, in a word, is man-shaped. Swedenborg's Grand Man, the Adam Kadmon of the Kabbalah, Blake's 'human face of God' are all expressions of the same insight that Milosz formulates when he writes that 'in Adam's thinking, all describable space—that is, all space susceptible to being situated experimentally in numerical relation between galaxies, systems, worlds and moving bodies in general—that describable space, together with movement and time, formed a single universal Body'. [11]   In *The Arcana* (a gesture perhaps to Swedenborg's *Arcana Caelestia*) Milosz writes that 'When the spirit of purity and obedience prompted the newborn Adam to rise from the ground so that he might bless the world's beauty, our ancestor *felt he was the Universe*'. [12] Milosz expressed this idea more immediately in a letter to a friend: 'God is a man', he wrote. 'That is why the Bible has that passionate tone not found in other religions dominated by metaphysics. God does not practise metaphysics.' [13]

Such ideas are considered the height of folly among mainstream scientists, proposing, as they do, a false centrality to human existence. Yet, in recent years, developments like the 'anthropic cosmological principle', first put forward by John Barrow and Frank Tipler in the 1980s, suggest, if not a Grand Man, then at least the notion that our human presence in the universe is not the result of mere chance, and that somehow, in our universe human existence is required.[14]

I might mention a further example of the similarity between Swedenborg and Milosz, one they share, I believe, with William Blake. As Czeslaw Milosz points out, Oscar Milosz was unaware of Blake's work, which is ironic when one sees how much Milosz's thought has in common with that of the great English poet. For Swedenborg, a central element of existence is what he calls 'use', the active employment of love and wisdom. This active character of being was expressed by Blake in his notion of 'contraries', the idea that being itself is maintained by the tension of opposing forces: 'Without contraries', he wrote, 'there is no progression'. (Goethe, too, shared this belief: 'In the beginning was the deed', he writes in *Faust*, and later philosophical schools, like *lebensphilosophie* (Bergson, Nietzsche) and existentialism, also shared an insistence on the centrality of 'action'.) This insight into the active nature of reality is expressed by Milosz in his remarks on 'movement', which for him is the key reality from which matter, space and time emerge. 'Movement precedes the thing. It is only thanks to movement that the thing is. For the thing is space and time given by movement.'[15] 'Thought', he wrote, 'is that act by which we situate all things in a safe place through awareness and love of movement'.[16] 'Man's first thought had been a total perception of his movement: an instantaneous awareness and *love*, a religious ecstasy of rhythm.'[17]

Like Swedenborg, Milosz believed in an historical unfolding of revelation, which Swedenborg described as a series of 'Churches'. Milosz considered himself the founder of the 6th such Church, and saw as his mission the renewal of Christian metaphysics and the annunciation of a future Christianity. He maintained that nothing of his mystical or metaphysical insights deviated in the slightest from received Catholic doctrine, a point on which he differs from Swedenborg. He often spoke of what he foresaw as the 'Catholic Church of tomorrow', and repeatedly remarked that he did not write for the readers of his day, but for the future: 'one should not expect much from our contemporaries' he opined gloomily. He did harbour ideas of political action, based on his mystical insights, and toward the end of his life, believed that the West was heading toward a great upheaval. 'When the Holy Spirit makes itself heard in Rome', he announced, 'the necessary men will be present to answer the call'.[18] Such political musings may strike us as dubious, yet what they were based upon was perhaps the central event of Milosz's life, and this again was something that clearly declared a profound sympathy with Swedenborg's teachings. On 14 December, 1914, Milosz had an experience which changed his life. His account of it in 'Epistle to Storge' begins: 'On the fourteenth of December, nineteen hundred and fourteen, at about eleven o'clock in the evening, in a state of perfect wakefulness, having said my prayer and meditated my daily verse from the Bible, I suddenly felt, without the slightest amazement, a completely unexpected change occurring in my whole body'. [19] Soon after his experience, which Czeslaw Milosz likens unto the mystical experience of the religious thinker Blaise Pascal, Milosz was visited by a friend. O Milosz had not been seen for weeks, and when the friend knocked on his door, the poet emerged and announced calmly to his visitor that 'I have seen the spiritual sun'. Mention of a 'spiritual sun' will be familiar to readers of Swedenborg. In *The True Christian Religion,* at §767, Swedenborg writes that 'The Lord is the Sun of the angelic heaven, and this Sun appears before the eyes of angels when they are in spiritual meditation. The same thing happens with a man in this world, in whom the Church abides, as to the sight of his spirit'. This 'sun' Milosz describes as a 'gigantic and reddish egg' which was 'hurled with extraordinary force into space'. It then became 'round and small' and 'turned into a golden lamp' which lowered itself close to him, then shot again into the distance where it grew in size and 'recovered its oval shape of an angelic sun'. A plain of gold, which Milosz associated with alchemical gold, opened before him, and a 'perfect, absolute immobility overtook the sun and clouds', which filled him with a sense of having achieved a 'supreme accomplishment', a 'definite calm' and a 'complete halt to all mental operations'. He felt he had arrived at a 'superhuman realization [...] the final Rhythm'. [20]

A second vision, coming sometime later, reads like one of the descriptions of Swedenborg's hells, with 'dark lakes, greenish and putrescent [...] stagnant and desolate' over which curved an iron bridge of 'hideous shape and frightening length'. Here Milosz found 'an immense, deserted plain enclosed by a hostile silent circle of high and watchful mountains'. 'A universe of terror, billions and billions of times more vast, more crowded and more scintillating than our sidereal sky' stretched over his head. The movement of these 'tormented cosmic systems' was accompanied by an 'odious criminal noise, the enemy of all meditation, of all composure'. The secret meaning of all this movement, he discovered, was that 'you must multiply and divide the infinite by the infinite during an eternity of eternities'. [21]

This nightmare of an immense, threatening blackness in which vast cosmic systems turn incessantly reminds us of William Blake's dark visions of the 'starry wheels' and, indeed, of Pascal's earlier confession that the 'silences of these empty spaces' terrified him. It was in reaction to this crushing cosmic emptiness—which, although heightened by Milosz's almost hallucinatory prose, is a faithful rendering of our own Newtonian universe—that Milosz attempted to, in his own words, find the 'place' of mankind. As his younger relative wrote: 'A man must abide somewhere, a physical roof over his head is not enough; his mind needs its bearings, its points of reference, vertically as well as horizontally'.[22] What Milosz saw in his dark vision was that the 'place' of mankind had been lost, annulled in the infinite emptiness of abstract space, where, in the words of one of his commentators, we 'proclaim ourselves sovereign for a day of a lump of matter sentenced to slow decay in the darkness of a death without beginning or end'.[23]

Such a predicament makes us truly lost in space. Recognition of this peril is, however, fairly recent.

In one of the notes collected in the posthumous *The Will to Power*, Friedrich Nietzsche remarked that ever since Copernicus, 'man has been rolling from the centre toward X'.[24] What Nietzsche meant is that with the demise of the ancient cosmos, in which human-kind and the earth had a definite *place*, we have been moving, both literally and spiritually, into a vast unknown. That unknown is the Newtonian universe of absolute space and time. Rather than a vast cathedral of celestial spheres, arcing over an earth situated at their centre—which was how the pre-Copernican mind envisioned the cosmos—space since Newton has meant an abstract infinite *extension* in all directions. Likewise, time in the Newtonian universe means eternal *succession*, a temporal parallel to abstract infinity. If you take the co-ordinates 'here' and 'now' and from them draw a line extending infinitely in any direction (which, by definition, you would have to continue for eternity) you will never reach an 'end'. If, let us say, you were able to continue that line for a billion years, the distance remaining would still be infinite—as infinite as when you began—just as the time remaining to continue it would still be eternal, with as much eternity left as when you started.

Now, for the business of day-to-day life, these considerations are negligible. But if you are like Milosz (and myself), they leave one with a nagging feeling that something is not quite right. I remember when I was about 10 or 11 scaring my cousin by telling him that space never ended. If you imagined a wall of some kind, billions of light years away, you were always left with the question of what was on the other side of the wall. And if you answered 'Nothing', that didn't solve the problem, as our idea of 'nothing' is of an emptiness, which is merely more 'space'. It didn't take long to realize, however, that if space didn't end it was equally impossible to imagine it going on forever. I remember imagining a space ship travelling for billions of years, trying to reach the end of the universe, only to find itself faced with the same infinite distance ahead of it, and behind, as well. But how, my adolescent mind wondered, could that be? Most of us grow out of these mind-numbing reflections. But a handful remain troubled by them. Milosz was one of that handful, and he had some esteemed company, like Swedenborg.

For Swedenborg, the problem was really an illusion. The visible, outer world, he taught, is a reflection of an invisible spiritual world. Space and time are the proper ways in which we perceive things in the natural world, but they are incapable of seeing things in their 'true', spiritual being. From space and time, he writes at §69 of his *Divine Love and Wisdom,* 'man in the natural world forms the ideas of his thought and thence of his understanding. If he remains in these ideas and does not raise his mind above them, he can never perceive anything spiritual and divine'. Space and time are 'states' for Swedenborg, well and proper for life in the natural world, but wholly out of place in dealing with the realities of being. Do not, he entreats us, at §51, 'confound your ideas [of the Divine] with time and space, for insofar as anything of time and space is present [...] you will not understand [...] For the Divine is not in time and space'. William Blake, Swedenborg's sometimes critical follower, expressed this message with characteristic brevity: When the doors of perception are cleansed, he said, we would see all things as they really are, infinite. We would see a world in a grain of sand and eternity in an hour. 'Every space larger than a red Globule of man's blood is Visionary, and is created by the Hammer of Los: And every space smaller than a Globule of Man's blood opens Into an Eternity of which this vegetable Earth is But a Shadow' (*Milton*). This is the true meaning of infinite and eternal: not unending, but *outside* space and time. What the Newtonian concept of the universe had done was to *identify* the infinite with space, creating, in

Milosz's words, the actual conditions of hell. Milosz's experience of the 'spiritual sun' showed him that in identifying space with the infinite, man had, literally, lost his place in the cosmos. Indeed, the cosmos *itself* had no place. The question 'Where is space?' dominated Milosz's consciousness. He found he could not answer it. And, given a Newtonian universe of abstract infinite extension, an answer to this question seems impossible. In such a universe, there is literally no 'where' for space to be. Everything is 'in' such a space, yet that space itself is 'in' nothing. Anything that could contain space would itself be merely an extension of the space it contains. In a universe without borders, there can be no 'place', as the distinctions 'here' and 'there' lose their meaning in an infinitely empty space, free of reference points.

One consequence of Milosz's mystical experience is that he threw himself into a study of Kabbalistic, hermetic, alchemical and mystical writings, including the work of Swedenborg which, he tells us, he was unaware of until that time. He also tells us that he began to study the then recent and relatively unknown work of Einstein, whose ideas about the relativity of space and time Milosz believed were an attempt to find a way out of the Newtonian nightmare. In both cases, Milosz was encouraged to find that others had come upon insights similar to his own. In *Ars Magna*, Milosz attempted to express his mystical vision into the nature of place, movement, rhythm and the fundamental need for human consciousness to 'situate' itself and to find the 'place of places', which, for Milosz, is the 'Love which moves the sun and stars'. In *The Arcana* Milosz creates a spiritual history, giving an account of creation and man's primeval fall. The physical, visible universe, Milosz tells us, is the result of an emanation of divine incorporeal light into 'the nothing', a state absent of fullness or the void, absent, indeed, of any of the spatial concepts through which we perceive the natural world. Through this discharge of incorporeal light—which Milosz likens to the circulation of blood as well as to the emission of semen—the Divine could perceive the world's beauty. Yet our fall into the hellish infinity of abstract space, he tells us, came about through what he calls 'Adam's prevarication', when the original, purely spiritual universe, was transformed in human thought into the universe of space, time and matter. Adam and Eve, bridegroom and bride, united in conjugial love, somehow became aware of that which separated them from each other and from God. (And all love, Milosz tells us, is an echo of their original love for each other.) Like Swedenborg, Milosz locates this primordial fault line in the awakening sense of self, the *proprium*, when Adam first spoke the name 'I'. The result is the world we know. Yet this universe, for Milosz, is not a 'place'. 'As in time there are wakefulness and sleep, so in instantaneity [the eternal 'now' of the Divine] the entirety of the universe is only a *state*, situated in its spiritual opposition to the *nothing*, to the *nothing* from which the void and the full, movement and time, are banished.'[25]

If Milosz's words about 'the nothing' remind us of the *Ain Soph* of the Kabbalah or the Pleroma of the Gnostics, they are also strangely reminiscent of the manner in which present-day cosmologists speak of the paradoxical 'time' before the hypothetical Big Bang —paradoxical because, arguing that time and space as we know it were created *with* the Big Bang, they assure us that in truth there was no 'before' prior to their creation. Their language is indeed different than Milosz's, but in concrete terms, there was in truth 'nothing' prior to this 'accidental' eruption of being. For Milosz 'the corporeal Water of space-time was not poured by the fiat into the receptacle of a prior void. The Stone of space-time was not thrown into a pre-existing void'.[26] There was literally 'no thing' before the creation, not even absence, not even emptiness. There was a state that our minds, driven by habit to think in terms of space and time, find difficult, if not impossible to imagine.

A reader interested in a fuller picture of Milosz's fascinating thought could do no better than to track down a copy of *The Noble Traveller: The Life and Writings of O V de L Milosz*, the most complete collection of Milosz's work translated into English to date. Aside from the metaphysical poems discussed here, there is a long introduction by Czeslaw Milosz and a foreword by Christopher Bamford; a selection of Milosz's other poetry; a detailed 'Bio-Chronology'; copious notes and a selection of photographs. Milosz saw as his mission nothing less than a renewal of spiritual consciousness; the dedication of *Ars Magna*, his first great metaphysical poem, is to 'Renaissance', which he refers to often as his 'spouse'. He wrote, he said, not for today, but for tomorrow. There was much work to be done. Although in his practical life he devoted enormous amounts of time and energy to helping create a better Europe, he felt convinced that 'the present attempts at moral, social and political renewal are doomed to failure'. This was because 'a sacrilegious and false concept of the physical universe has dimmed, like a cataract, the intellectual sight of man'. Before the work of renewal could begin, he argued that it was 'necessary first to remove with a strong and charitable hand this opaque secretion which conceals [...] the real world of vision'.[27] Then, Milosz believed, we could begin to fulfil our destiny, which, he tells us, is to 'live and love eternally'. And then, he said, we can truly find our place, which 'is in the one who breathed into the nothing the ecstatic mirage of the world's beauty'.[28]

Some measure of that beauty can be found in Milosz's difficult but exceedingly inspiring poems. In their attempt to locate our 'place' in the cosmos, they are an expression of another mystical poet, Novalis', insight, one that Milosz truly felt, that 'all philosophy is homesickness'.

NOTES

[1] For a biographical essay on O Milosz, see my *Dedalus Book of the Occult: A Dark Muse* (Sawtry: Dedalus, 2003).

[2] Czeslaw Milosz, Introduction to *The Noble Traveller: The Life and Writings of O V de L Milosz* (West Stockbridge, MA: Lindisfarne, 1985), p. 18.

[3] Christopher Bamford, Foreword, ibid., p. 50.

[4] Czeslaw Milosz, ibid., p. 22.

[5] Milosz's novel *L'Amoureuse Initiation* (1910) is set in the Venice of the late 18th century.

[6] Goethe was a statesman; Novalis was an inspector of the Saxon salt mines; E T A Hoffmann was a jurist and held a seat on the Prussian Supreme Court.

[7] O Milosz, letter to Christian Gauss, *The Noble Traveller*, p. 440.

[8] Milosz adopted de Lubicz, not as another family name, but as a reference to an heraldic coat of arms, shared by many families belonging to the same clan. In 1919, O Milosz bestowed the honour of belonging to this clan to the alchemist and Egyptologist R A Schwaller, best known today as an early exponent of the belief that the Sphinx is many centuries older than the official archaeological assessment. For more on Milosz and Schwaller, see A VandenBroeck *Al Kemi: Hermetic, Occult, Political, and Private Aspects of R A Schwaler de Lubicz* (Hudson, NY: Lindisfarne Press, 1987).

[9] O Milosz, *The Noble Traveller*, p. 236.

[10] Ibid., p. 240; p. 403.

[11] Ibid., p. 280.

[12] Ibid., p. 278.

[13] Quoted in Czeslaw Milosz, *The Land of Ulro* (Manchester: Carcanet, 1985), p. 209.

[14] The anthropic cosmological principle argues that our universe is one in which the appearance of intelligent life forms, like ourselves, is possible, which seems a tautology; the strong version of the principle, however, goes further and argues that our universe is such that intelligent life forms like ourselves *had* to appear. Rather than products of chance, given the kind of universe we have, we were unavoidable.

[15] O Milosz, *The Noble Traveller*, p. 264.

[16] Ibid., p. 240.

[17] Ibid., p. 278.

[18] Ibid., p. 372. Milosz put some of his ideas into practice in the years following World War I, when he, along with other esotericists, including Rene Schwaller, became involved in a right-wing political organization, *Les Veillieurs*. For more on this, see A VandenBroeck's *Al Kemi* mentioned above.

[19] O Milosz, *The Noble Traveller*, p. 244.

[20] Ibid., p. 245.

[21] Ibid., pp. 246-7.

[22] Czeslaw Milosz, *The Land of Ulro*, p. 152.

[23] Philip Sherrard, *Human Image: World Image* (Ipswich: Golgonooza Press, 1992), p. 134.

[24] Friedrich Nietzsche, *The Will to Power*, ed. Walter Kaufmann (New York: Random House, 1967), p. 8.

[25] O Milosz, *The Noble Traveller*, p. 281.

[26] Ibid., p. 282.

[27] Ibid., p. 285.

[28] Ibid., p. 282.

The Story of Swedenborg[1]

Arthur Conan Doyle

I t is impossible to give any date for the early appearances of external intelligent power of a higher or lower type impinging upon the affairs of men. Spiritualists are in the habit of taking March 31, 1848, as the beginning of all psychic things, because their own movement dates from that day.[2] There has, however, been no time in the recorded history of the world when we do not find traces of preternatural interference and a tardy recognition of them from humanity. The only difference between these episodes and the modern movement is that the former might be described as a case of stray wanderers from some further sphere, while the latter bears the sign of a purposeful and organized invasion. But as an invasion might well be preceded by the appearance of pioneers who search out the land, so the spirit influx of recent years was heralded by a number of incidents which might well be traced to the Middle Ages or beyond them. Some term must be fixed for a commencement of the narrative, and perhaps no better one can be found than the story of the great Swedish seer, Emanuel Swedenborg, who has some claim to be the father of our new knowledge of supernal matters.

When the first rays of the rising sun of spiritual knowledge fell upon the earth they illuminated the greatest and highest human mind before they shed their light on lesser men. That mountain peak of mentality was this great religious reformer and clairvoyant medium, as little understood by his own followers as ever the Christ has been.

In order fully to understand Swedenborg one would need to have a Swedenborg brain, and that is not met with once in a century. And yet by our power of comparison and our experience of facts of which Swedenborg knew nothing, we can realize some part of his life more clearly than he could himself. The object of this study is not to treat the man as a whole, but to endeavour to place him in the general scheme of psychic unfolding treated in this work, from which his own Church in its narrowness would withhold him.[3]

Swedenborg was a contradiction in some ways to our psychic generalizations, for it has been the habit to say that great intellect stands in the way of personal psychic experience. The clean slate is certainly most apt for the writing of a message. Swedenborg's mind was no clean slate, but was criss-crossed with every kind of exact learning which mankind is capable of acquiring. Never was there such a concentration of information. He was primarily a great mining engineer and authority on metallurgy. He was a military engineer who helped to turn the fortunes of one of the many campaigns of Charles XII of Sweden.[4] He was a great authority upon astronomy and physics, the author of learned works upon the tides and the determination of latitude.[5] He was a zoologist and an anatomist. He was a financier and political economist who anticipated the conclusions of Adam Smith.[6] Finally, he was a profound Biblical student who had sucked in theology with his mother's milk, and lived in the stern Evangelical atmosphere of a Lutheran pastor during the most impressionable years of his life. His psychic development, which occurred when he was fifty-five, in no way interfered with his mental activity, and several of his scientific pamphlets were published after that date.[7]

With such a mind it is natural enough that he should be struck by the evidence for extra-mundane powers which comes in the way of every thoughtful man, but what is not natural is that he should himself be the medium for such powers. There is a sense in which his mentality was actually detrimental and vitiated his results, and there was another in which it was to the highest degree useful. To illustrate this one has to consider the two categories into which his work may be divided.

The first is the theological. This seems to most people outside the chosen flock a useless and perilous side of his work. On the one hand he accepts the Bible as being in a very particular sense the work of God. Upon the other he contends that its true meaning is entirely different from its obvious meaning, and that it is he, and only he, who, by the help of angels, is able to give the true meaning. Such a claim is intolerable. The infallibility of the Pope would be a trifle compared with the infallibility of Swedenborg if such a position were admitted. The Pope is at least only infallible when giving his verdict on points of doctrine *ex cathedra* with his cardinals around him. Swedenborg's infallibility would be universal and unrestricted. Nor do his explanations in the least commend themselves to one's reason. When, in order to get at the true sense of a God-given message, one has to suppose that a horse signifies intellectual truth, an ass signifies scientific truth, a flame signifies improvement, and so on and on through countless symbols,[8] we seem to be in a realm of make-believe which can only be compared with the ciphers which some ingenious critics have detected in the plays of Shakespeare. Not thus does God send His truth into the world. If such a view were accepted the Swedenborgian creed could only be the mother of a thousand heresies, and we should find ourselves back again amid the hair-splittings and the syllogisms of the mediaeval schoolmen. All great and true things are simple and intelligible. Swedenborg's theology is neither simple nor intelligible, and that is its condemnation.

When, however, we get behind his tiresome exegesis of the Scriptures, where everything means something different from what it obviously means, and when we get at some of the general results of his teaching, they are not inharmonious with liberal modern thought or with the teaching which has been received from the Other Side since spiritual communication became open. Thus the general proposition that this world is a laboratory of souls, a forcing-ground where the material refines out the spiritual, is not to be disputed. He rejects the Trinity in its ordinary sense, but rebuilds it in some extraordinary sense which would be equally objectionable to a Unitarian. He admits that every system has its divine purpose and that virtue is not confined to Christianity. He agrees with the Spiritualist teaching in seeking the true meaning of Christ's life in its power as an example, and he rejects atonement and original sin. He sees the root of all evil in selfishness, yet he admits that a healthy egoism, as Hegel called it, is essential. In sexual matters his theories are liberal to the verge of laxity. A Church he considered an absolute necessity, as if no individual could arrange his own dealings with his Creator. Altogether, it is such a jumble of ideas, poured forth at such length in so many great Latin volumes, and expressed in so obscure a style, that every independent interpreter of it would be liable to found a new religion of his own. Not in that direction does the worth of Swedenborg lie.

That worth is really to be found in his psychic powers and in his psychic information which would have been just as valuable had no word of theology ever come from his pen. It is these powers and that information to which we will now turn.

Even as a lad young Swedenborg had visionary moments,[9] but the extremely practical and energetic manhood which followed submerged that more delicate side of his nature. It came occasionally to the surface, however, all through his life, and several instances have been put on record which show that he possessed those powers which are usually called 'travelling clairvoyance', where the soul appears to leave the body, to acquire information at a distance, and to return with news of what is occurring elsewhere. It is a not uncommon attribute of mediums, and can be matched by a thousand examples among Spiritualistic sensitives, but it is rare in people of intellect, and rare also when accompanied by an apparently normal state of the body while the phenomenon is proceeding. Thus, in the oft-quoted example of Gothenburg, where the seer observed and reported on a fire in Stockholm, 300 miles away, with perfect accuracy, he was at a dinner-party with sixteen guests, who made valuable witnesses. The story was investigated by no less a person than the philosopher Kant, who was a contemporary.[10]

These occasional incidents were, however, merely the signs of latent powers which came to full fruition quite suddenly in London in April of the year 1744.[11] It may be remarked that though the seer was of a good Swedish family and was elevated to the Swedish nobility, it was none the less in London that his chief books were published, that his illumination was begun and finally that he died and was buried.[12] From the day of his first vision he continued until his death, twenty-seven years later, to be in constant touch with the other world.

The same night the world of spirits, hell and heaven, were convincingly opened to me, where I found many persons of my acquaintance of all conditions. Thereafter the Lord daily opened the eyes of my spirit to see in perfect wakefulness what was going on in the other world, and to converse, broad awake, with angels and spirits.[13]

In his first vision Swedenborg speaks of 'a kind of vapour steaming from the pores of my body. It was a most visible watery vapour and fell downwards to the ground upon the carpet'.[14] This is a close description of that ectoplasm which we have found to be the basis of all physical phenomena. The substance has also been called 'ideoplasm', because it takes on in an instant any shape with which it is impressed by the spirit. In this case it changed, according to his account, into vermin, which was said to be a sign from his Guardians that they disapproved of his diet, and was accompanied by a clairaudient warning that he must be more careful in that respect.[15]

What can the world make of such a narrative? They may say that the man was mad, but his life in the years which followed showed no sign of mental weakness. Or they might say that he lied. But he was a man who was famed for his punctilious veracity. His friend Cuno, a banker of Amsterdam, said of him, 'When he gazed upon me with his smiling blue eyes it was as if truth itself was speaking from them'.[16] Was he then self-deluded and honestly mistaken? We have to face the fact that in the main the spiritual observations which he made have been confirmed and extended since his time by innumerable psychic observers. The true verdict is that he was the first and in many ways the greatest of the whole line of mediums, that he was subject to the errors as well as to the privileges which mediumship brings, that only by the study of mediumship can his powers be really understood, and that in endeavouring to separate him from Spiritualism his New Church has shown a complete misapprehension of his gifts, and of their true place in the general scheme of Nature. As a great pioneer of the Spiritual movement his position is both intelligible and glorious. As an isolated figure with incomprehensible powers, there is no place for him in any broad comprehensive scheme of religious thought.

It is interesting to note that he considered his powers to be intimately connected with a system of respiration. Air and ether being all around us, it is as if some men could breathe more ether and less air and so attain a more etheric state.[17] This, no doubt, is a crude and clumsy way of putting it, but some such idea runs through the work of many schools of psychic thought. Laurence Oliphant, who had no obvious connexion with Swedenborg, wrote his book *Sympneumata* in order to explain it.[18] The Indian system of Yoga depends upon the same idea. But anyone who has seen an ordinary medium go into trance is aware of the peculiar hissing intakes with which the process begins and the deep expirations with which it ends. A fruitful field of study lies there for the Science of the future. Here, as in other psychic matters, caution is needed. The author has known several cases where tragic results have followed upon an ignorant use of deep-breathing psychic exercises. Spiritual, like electrical power, has its allotted use, but needs some knowledge and caution in handling.

Swedenborg sums up the matter by saying that when he communed with spirits he would for an hour at a time hardly draw a breath, 'taking in only enough air to serve as a supply to his thoughts'.[19] Apart from this peculiarity of respiration, Swedenborg was normal during his visions, though he naturally preferred to be secluded at such times. He seems to have been privileged to examine the other world through several of its spheres, and though his theological habit of mind may have tinctured his descriptions, on the other hand the vast range of his material knowledge gave him unusual powers of observation and comparison. Let us see what were the main facts which he brought back from his numerous journeys, and how far they coincide with those which have been obtained since his day by psychic methods.

He found, then, that the other world, to which we all go after death, consisted of a number of different spheres representing various shades of luminosity and happiness, each of us going to that for which our spiritual condition has fitted us. We are judged in automatic fashion, like going to like by some spiritual law, and the result being determined by the total result of our life, so that absolution or a death-bed repentance can be of little avail. He found in these spheres that the scenery and conditions of this world were closely reproduced, and so also was the general framework of society. He found houses in which families lived, temples in which they worshipped, halls in which they assembled for social purposes, palaces in which rulers might dwell.

Death was made easy by the presence of celestial beings who helped the newcomer into his fresh existence. Such newcomers had an immediate period of complete rest. They regained consciousness in a few days of our time.

There were both angels and devils, but they were not of another order to ourselves. They were all human beings who had lived on earth and who were either undeveloped souls, as devils, or highly developed souls, as angels.

We did not change in any way at death. Man lost nothing by death, but was still a man in all respects, though more perfect than when in the body. He took with him not only his powers but also his acquired modes of thought, his beliefs and his prejudices.

All children were received equally, whether baptized or not. They grew up in the other world. Young women mothered them until the real mother came across.

There was no eternal punishment. Those who were in the hells could work their way out if they had the impulse. Those in the heavens were also in no permanent place, but were working their way to something higher.

There was marriage in the form of spiritual union in the next world. It takes a man and a woman to make a complete human unit. Swedenborg, it may be remarked, was never married in life.

There was no detail too small for his observation in the spirit spheres. He speaks of the architecture, the artisans' work, the flowers and fruits, the scribes, the embroidery, the art, the music, the literature, the science, the schools, the museums, the colleges, the libraries and the sports. It may all shock conventional minds, though why harps, crowns and thrones should be tolerated and other less material things denied, it is hard to see.

Those who left this world old, decrepit, diseased, or deformed, renewed their youth, and gradually assumed their full vigour. Married couples continued together if their feelings towards each other were close and sympathetic. If not, the marriage was dissolved.

> Two real lovers are not separated by the death of one, since the spirit of the deceased dwells with the spirit of the survivor, and this even to the death of the latter, when they again meet and are reunited, and love each other more tenderly than before.[20]

Such are some gleanings out of the immense store of information which God sent to the world through Swedenborg. Again and again they have been repeated by the mouths and the pens of our own Spiritualistic illuminates. The world has so far disregarded it, and clung to outworn and senseless conceptions. Gradually the new knowledge is making its way, however, and when it has been entirely accepted the true greatness of the mission of Swedenborg will be recognized, while his Biblical exegesis will be forgotten.

The New Church, which was formed in order to sustain the teaching of the Swedish master, has allowed itself to become a backwater instead of keeping its rightful place as the original source of psychic knowledge. When the Spiritualistic movement broke out in 1848, and when men like Andrew Jackson Davis supported it with philosophic writings and psychic powers which can hardly be distinguished from those of Swedenborg,[21] the New Church would have been well advised to hail this development as being on the lines indicated by their leader. Instead of doing so, they have preferred, for some reason which is difficult to understand, to exaggerate every point of difference and ignore every point of resemblance, until the two bodies have drifted into a position of hostility. In point of fact, every Spiritualist should honour Swedenborg, and his bust should be in every Spiritualist temple, as being the first and greatest of modern mediums. On the other hand, the New Church should sink any small differences and join heartily in the new movement, contributing their churches and organization to the common cause.

It is difficult on examining Swedenborg's life to discover what are the causes which make his present-day followers look askance at other psychic bodies. What he did then is what they do now. Speaking of Polhem's death the seer says:

He died on Monday and spoke with me on Thursday. I was invited to the funeral. He saw the hearse and saw them let down the coffin into the grave. He conversed with me as it was going on, asking me why they had buried him when he was alive. When the priest pronounced that he would rise again at the Day of Judgment he asked why this was, when he had risen already. He wondered that such a belief could obtain, considering that he was even now alive.[22]

This is entirely in accord with the experience of a present-day medium. If Swedenborg was within his rights, then the medium is so also.

Again: 'Brahe was beheaded at 10 in the morning and spoke to me at 10 that night. He was with me almost without interruption for several days'.[23]

Such instances show that Swedenborg had no more scruples about converse with the dead than the Christ had when He spoke on the mountain with Moses and Elias.[24]

Swedenborg has laid down his own view very clearly, but in considering it one has to remember the time in which he lived and his want of experience of the trend and object of the new revelation. This view was that God, for good and wise purposes, had separated the world of spirits from ours and that communication was not granted except for cogent reasons—among which mere curiosity should not be counted. Every earnest student of the psychic would agree with it, and every earnest Spiritualist is averse from turning the most solemn thing upon earth into a sort of pastime. As to having a cogent reason, our main reason is that in such an age of materialism as Swedenborg can never have imagined, we are endeavouring to prove the existence and supremacy of spirit in so objective a way that it will meet and beat the materialists on their own ground. It would be hard to imagine any reason more cogent than this, and therefore we have every right to claim that if Swedenborg were now living he would have been a leader in our modern psychic movement.

Some of his followers, notably Dr Garth Wilkinson, have put forward another objection thus: 'The danger of man in speaking with spirits is that we are all in association with our likes, and being full of evil these similar spirits, could we face them, would but confirm us in our own state of views'. [25]

To this we can only reply that though it is specious it is proved by experience to be false. Man is not naturally bad. The average human being is good. The mere act of spiritual communication in its solemnity brings out the religious side. Therefore as a rule it is not the evil but the good influence which is encountered, as the beautiful and moral records of séances will show. The author can testify that in nearly forty years of psychic work, during which he has attended innumerable séances in many lands, he has never on any single occasion heard an obscene word or any message which could offend the ears of the most delicate female. Other veteran Spiritualists bring the same testimony. Therefore, while it is undoubtedly true that evil spirits are attracted to an evil circle, in actual practice it is a very rare thing for anyone to be incommoded thereby. When such spirits come the proper procedure is not to repulse them, but rather to reason gently with them and so endeavour to make them realize their own condition and what they should do for self-improvement. This has occurred many times within the author's personal experience and with the happiest results.

Some little personal account of Swedenborg may fitly end this brief review of his doctrines, which is primarily intended to indicate his position in the general scheme. He must have been a most frugal, practical, hard-working and energetic young man, and a most lovable old one. Life seems to have mellowed him into a very gentle and venerable creature. He was placid, serene, and ever ready for conversation which did not take a psychic turn unless his companions so desired. The material of such conversations was always remarkable, but he was afflicted with a stammer which hindered his enunciation.[26] In person he was tall and spare, with a spiritual face, blue eyes, a wig to his shoulders, dark clothing, knee-breeches, buckles, and a cane.

Swedenborg claimed that a heavy cloud was formed round the earth by the psychic grossness of humanity, and that from time to time there was a judgment and a clearing up, even as the thunderstorm clears the material atmosphere. He saw that the world, even in his day, was drifting into a dangerous position owing to the unreason of the Churches on the one side and the reaction towards absolute want of religion which was caused by it.[27] Modern psychic authorities, notably Vale Owen, have spoken of this ever-accumulating cloud, and there is a very general feeling that the necessary cleansing process will not be long postponed.[28]

A notice of Swedenborg from the Spiritualistic standpoint may be best concluded by an extract from his own diary. He says: 'All confirmations in matters pertaining to theology are, as it were, glued fast into the brains, and can with difficulty be removed, and while they remain, genuine truths can find no place'.[29] He was a very great seer, a great pioneer of psychic knowledge, and his weakness lay in those very words which he has written.

The general reader who desires to go further will find Swedenborg's most characteristic teachings in his *Heaven and Hell*, *The New Jerusalem* and *Arcana Caelestia*. His life has been admirably done by Garth Wilkinson, Trobridge, and Brayley Hodgetts, the present president of the English Swedenborg Society.[30] In spite of all his theological symbolism, his name must live eternally as the first of all modern men who has given a description of the process of death, and of the world beyond, which is not founded upon the vague ecstatic and impossible visions of the old Churches, but which actually corresponds with the descriptions which we ourselves obtain from those who endeavour to convey back to us some clear idea of their new existence.

NOTES

[1] This essay first appeared as the opening chapter of Doyle's *The History of Spiritualism*, vol.

I (1926). 'The Story of Swedenborg' was not written with the intention of placing it at the beginning of a history, as Doyle explains in his preface:

This genesis needs some little explanation. I had written certain studies with no particular ulterior object save to gain myself, and to pass on to others, a clear view of what seemed to me to be important episodes in the modern spiritual development of the human race. These included the chapters on Swedenborg.

[2] In Hydesville, a village outside Rochester in New York State, lived the Fox family, farmers who experienced rapping sounds in their home in 1848. Doyle explains the importance of this particular date for Spiritualists in chapter IV, 'The Hydesville Episode', of *The History of Spiritualism*, vol. I.

[3] Swedenborg never established his own church.

[4] Swedenborg met Charles XII (1682-1718, King of Sweden from 1697), who appointed him assessor of the Royal Board of Mines, in 1716. In 1718 Swedenborg assisted Charles XII's siege of Frederikshall with an invention of a machine that was able to transport boats a distance of fourteen miles over land from Strömstad to Iddefjord.

[5] Swedenborg was the author of *Försök at finna östra och westra lengden igen, igenom månan, som til the lärdas ompröfwande framstelles* [Attempt to find the east and west longitude by means of the moon, which is submitted for the reconsideration of the learned] (Uppsala, 1718) which was reprinted with alterations from an article first published in the scientific journal he wrote and edited with Christopher Polhem, *Daedalus Hyperboreus*, issue 4 (Uppsala, 1716); *On the Height of Water and Strong Tides in the primeval world* [*Om wattens högd, och förra werldens starcka ebb och flod*, Uppsala, 1719], tr. J E Rosenquist, in *Scientific and Philosophical Treatises* (Bryn Athyn, 1992); *A New Method of Finding the Longitude of Places, on Land or at Sea, by Lunar Observations* [*Methodus Nova Inveniendi Longitudines Locorum Terra Marique ope Lunae*, Amsterdam, 1721, publ. anon.], tr. C E Strutt, in *Some Specimens of a Work on the Principles of Chemistry, with other treatises by Emanuel Swedenborg* (London, 1847; Bryn Athyn, 1976).

[6] Swedenborg's works on anatomy and the search to locate the soul in the body include *The Economy of the Animal Kingdom* [*Oeconomia Regni Animalis*, 2 vols., Amsterdam & London, 1740-1, publ. anon.], tr. A Clissold, 2 vols. (London, 1845-6), *The Animal Kingdom* [*Regnum Animale*, 3 vols., vols. I-II The Hague, 1744; vol. III London, 1745], tr. J J G Wilkinson, 2 vols. (London, 1843-4) and the posthumously published *The Cerebrum* [*Transactiones de Cerebro*, w. 1738-40], tr. A Acton, 2 vols. (Bryn Athyn, 1976). The titles of the first two works perhaps misled Doyle, Swedenborg wrote about the natural world in his philosophy and as a mineralogist, but he was not a zoologist. As a political economist, Doyle is perhaps thinking of Swedenborg's *Förslag til vårt mynts och måls Indelning, så at räkningen kan lättas och alt bråk afskaffas* [Proposal to divide our money and measures, so that the calculation would be easy and all fractions be abolished] (Uppsala, 1719) and, in particular, his *Modest Thoughts on Inflation*

of Swedish Currency [*Oförgripelige tanckar om swenska myntetz förnedring och förhögning*, Stockholm, 1722; Enlarged edition, Uppsala, 1771], tr. A Acton & B A H Boyeson, rev. & ed. G Dole, in *Studia Swedenborgia*, vol. VI (Jan. 1987). Swedenborg also submitted a *Memorial on the Balance of Trade* to the Swedish Diet in 1723, a translation of which can be found in *The Letters and Memorials of Emanuel Swedenborg*, tr. A Acton, 2 vols. (Bryn Athyn, 1948-55), vol. II, pp. 289-96. Swedenborg was a member of the Swedish House of Nobles, first taking his seat there on his family's ennoblement in 1719, and he attended regularly up until his death, usually remaining in Sweden whilst the Diet was in session.

Adam Smith (1723-90). Scottish economist and philosopher and author of *Theory of Moral Sentiments* (1759) and *An Inquiry into the Nature and Causes of the Wealth of the Nations* (1776) which established economics as its own subject and conceived of the doctrine of free enterprise.

[7] 1743 is widely recognized as the year that Swedenborg received his spiritual enlightenment. He did indeed publish his *The Animal Kingdom* [*Regnum Animale*] in The Hague (vols. I-II) and London (vol. III) in 1744-5, but aside from a small treatise on *Inlaying Marble Tables* (1763), he was primarily concerned with his theological works, only re-issuing editions of scientific works.

[8] See, for example, Swedenborg, *Arcana Caelestia*, §574.2: ' "horses" here and elsewhere in the Word stands for the rational'; ibid. §2781.1: ' "a wild ass" means rational truth separated from good [...] and "an ass" factual knowledge in particular'; and ibid., §6601: 'a glowing flame corresponds to an affection for good'.

[9] Cf. Swedenborg in his letter to G A Beyer, November 14, 1769, in Alfred Acton (tr. and ed.) *The Letters and Memorials of Emanuel Swedenborg*, vol. II, p. 696: 'From my 4th to my 10th year, I was constantly in thought concerning God, salvation, and the *spiritual sufferings* of men, and several times revealed that at which my father and mother wondered, saying that angels must be speaking through me'.

[10] German philosopher Immanuel Kant (1724-1804) wrote about the Gothenburg fire anecdote, which happened in 1759, in his *Dreams of a Spirit-Seer Elucidated through Dreams of Metaphysics* (1766) and in a letter to Charlotte von Knobloch, August 10, 1763, both of which can be found in *Kant on Swedenborg: Dreams of a Spirit-Seer and Other Writings*, tr. Gregory R Johnson and Glenn Alexander Magee (Pennsylvania: Swedenborg Foundation, 2002), pp. 43-4 and 70-1 respectively.

[11] Doyle means April 1745, when Swedenborg had a vision in a London inn. This was not, as Doyle goes on to state, Swedenborg's 'first vision', he had been having a series of visions and dreams across 1744-5, recorded in his *Journal of Dreams*, including one in April 1744, when he was in Delft, Holland.

[12] Swedenborg was buried in 1772 at London's first Swedish Church (where he had worshipped during his visits) in Prince's Square, East London. In 1908 his remains were removed for re-

interment at Uppsala Cathedral in Sweden. The church at Prince's Square closed in 1921, and the Square was renamed Swedenborg Gardens in 1938.

[13] Cf. 'Robsahm's Memoirs of Swedenborg', Document no. 5, in R L Tafel (tr., ed. and comp.), *Documents concerning the Life and Character of Emanuel Swedenborg*, 3 vols. (London, 1875-7), vol. I, p. 36.

[14] Cf. Swedenborg, *Spiritual Diary*, §397.

[15] Cf. 'Robsahm's Memoirs of Swedenborg' in R L Tafel (tr., ed. and comp.), *Documents...*, vol. I, p. 35; and Swedenborg, *Spiritual Diary*, §397.

[16] 'Cuno's Experience', Document no. 256, in R L Tafel (tr., ed. and comp.) *Documents...*, vol. II:1, p. 445.

[17] See Swedenborg, *Spiritual Diary*, §3464.

[18] Laurence Oliphant (1829-88), English writer and lawyer. His book *Sympneumata: Evolutionary Forces now Active in Man* (1885) was written with his first wife, Alice Le Strange, and supposedly dictated by a spirit.

[19] Cf. Swedenborg, *Spiritual Diary*, §3464: 'I sometimes scarcely breathed by inspiration at all for the space of a short hour, and merely drew in enough of air to keep up the process of thinking.'

[20] Swedenborg, *Conjugial Love*, §321.7.

[21] Andrew Jackson Davis (1826-1910), American author, mesmerist and spiritualist. He wrote many books about his trance revelations and tried to provide an intellectual framework for Spiritualism. Davis claimed to have received dictations and advice from Swedenborg.

[22] Swedenborg, *Spiritual Diary (Minor)*, §4752. Christopher Polhem or Pålhammar (1661-1751) was a Swedish scientist whom Swedenborg assisted at his mechanical institution in Stjersund in Dalecarlia and collaborated with on the periodical *Daedalus Hyperboreus*.

[23] Swedenborg, *Spiritual Diary,* §5099. Count Erik Brahe (1722-56), Swedish nobleman who was a colonel in the army. He was one of the leaders in a failed Royalist coup in 1756 and was executed by order of the Hat party in 1756.

[24] Mark 9.4.

[25] Dr James John Garth Wilkinson (1812-99) was a homeopathic doctor, social reformer, author and a Swedenborgian scholar and translator. The quoted phrase is untraced.

[26] Swedenborg mentions a speech impediment in a letter to Eric Benzelius, May 26, 1724, which can be found in A Acton, *Letters and Memorials*, vol. I, p. 334: 'I have not the *donum docendi* [the gift of teaching], as my Brother knows, by reason of the *naturella difficultate* of speech.'. For other references to Swedenborg's impediment in speech see: R L Tafel (tr., ed. and comp.), *Documents...*, vol. I, pp. 34, 57, vol. II:1, p. 545 and vol. II:2, p. 696.

[27] Cf. Swedenborg, *Coronis*, summary IX-XIV.

[28] Revd George Vale Owen (1860-1931). Vicar of Orford, Lancashire, and Spiritualist author of such works as *The Life Beyond the Veil* (1920)—to which Doyle wrote an introduction—*Paul*

and Albert (1924)and *Body, Soul and Spirit* (1928) which were the results of automatic writing.

[29] The quotation is not in fact from either Swedenborg's *Spiritual Diary* or his *Journal of Dreams*, but is, rather, from a letter to G A Beyer, 25 September, 1766, which can be found in A Acton (tr. & ed.), *Letters and Memorials*, vol. II, p. 622.

[30] J J Garth Wilkinson, *Emanuel Swedenborg: A Biographical Sketch* (London: William Newberry, 1849; 2nd edn. London: James Speirs, 1886); George Trobridge (1851-1909), *Emanuel Swedenborg, his Life, Teachings, and Influence* (London: Frederick Warne & Co., 1907; 4th edn. rev. E C Mongredion, London: Swedenborg Society, 1935); Edward Arthur Brayley Hodgetts (1859-1932, president of the Swedenborg society 1921-3), *Reasonable Religion. Emanuel Swedenborg His Message & Teaching* (London & Toronto: J M Dent & Sons, Ltd., 1923).

Biographies

Index

Biographies

Charles Baudelaire was born in 1821, the only child of François Baudelaire and his second wife Caroline Defayis. He began writing poetry as a student and attended the Collège Royale Lyon (1832-6), the Lycée Louis-le-grand (1836-9) and later studied law at the Ecole de Droit. His father died in 1827 and his mother married Jacques Aspic, who sent Baudelaire on a voyage to India in June 1841 in an attempt to draw him away from his increasingly indulgent lifestyle. Charles jumped ship in Mauritius and returned to France in 1842. In 1847 he published his first novel, the auto-biographical *La Fanfarlo,* and co-founded the journal *Le Salut Public*. In 1848 he became involved in politics and fought on the barricades during the revolution. From 1852-65 he was occupied with the translation of Edgar Allan Poe's writings. His *Les Fleurs Du Mal* was published in 1857 with the result that all those involved with its publishing were found guilty of obscenity and blasphemy. A second edition was publish-ed in 1861, establishing Baudelaire as one of the great French poets of the 19th century. Baudelaire was interested in what is beyond and around us, which he promoted in his Swedenborgian influenced sonnet 'Les correspondances'. In 1862 he suffered a minor stroke and his health deteriorated due to his excessive lifestyle. In 1863 a collection of his criticism under the title *Le Peintre de la Vie Moderne* was published. He died, in poverty, on August 31, 1867.

Joseph Sheridan Le Fanu was born in Dublin in 1814 into a noble family of Huguenot origin. His grandmother, Alice Sheridan Le Fanu, and her brother Richard Brinsley Sheridan were both playwrights while his father was a clergyman. Educated at Trinity College Dublin, he was called to the Bar but found little success in legal practice. He earned his living as a journalist, newspaper proprietor, short story writer and novelist. He married Susanna Bennett in 1843 and they had four children. Susanna died shortly before her thirty-fifth birthday. A keen reader of Swedenborg, he is famous for his tales of mystery and the supernatural. His best-known novel, *Uncle Silas* (1864), has a leading character who is a Swedenborgian. Other works include *The Wyvern Mystery* (1869) and the remarkable collection of stories, *In a Glass Darkly* (1872). The latter includes 'Carmilla', a tale of vampirism set in Austria (not Transylvania) which anticipates Bram Stoker's *Dracula* by exactly a quarter of a century, and 'Green Tea' which contains several quotations from Swedenborg's *Arcana Caelestia*. Le Fanu died in Dublin in 1873.

Ernest Theodor Amadeus (originally Wilhelm) ***Hoffmann*** was born in 1776, in Königsberg, Prussia. He changed his name to Amadeus in 1813 in honour of the composer Wolfgang Amadeus Mozart. At the university of Königsberg he followed his father's career as a lawyer. He later started work as a Prussian Law officer in Berlin, Poland and Brandenburg (among other places) but was accused of spying by the Prussian King. As a result he moved, in 1805, to Berlin to pursue his artistic life working as a conductor, critic and theatrical musical director. Realizing he would never be a great composer he turned to writing. In 1809, he published his first literary work, and the first of his unusual works connected to music, 'Ritter Gluck' in which a mad musician is possessed with the idea that he is the composer Gluck. His struggle between artistic life and a legal career is reflected in his story 'Das Fräulein von Scuderi' (Mademoiselle Scudery, 1819) about a goldsmith, a highly respected citizen, who becomes at night a criminal, and he went on to write numerous short stories which have since influenced authors as diverse as Franz Kafka, Edgar Allan Poe, Charles Dickens and Nikolai Gogol. Hoffman's writing also had a direct influence on Delibes's ballet *Coppélia* and Tchaikovsky's *Nutcracker*. English editions of Hoffman's work includes *The Devil's Elixirs* (1963), *Selected Writings of E T A Hoffmann* (1969) and *Tales of E T A Hoffmann* (1972). Hoffmann died in Berlin on June 25, 1822.

George MacDonald was born in Aberdeenshire in December 1824 to devout Calvinist parents and was educated at the University of Aberdeen. He came to London to train as a minister of the Congregational Church and held his first and only pastorate at Arundel, Sussex. He married Louisa Powell in 1851 and they had eleven children. Resigning his pastorate after the 'advanced' German theology he preached was unpopular, he lived thereafter by writing, lecturing and lay preaching. A poet and prolific novelist, he is remembered particularly for his fantasies, *At the Back of the North Wind* (1871), *The Princess and the Goblin* (1872), *The Princess and Curdie* (1883), *Phantastes* (1858) and *Lilith* (1895). These books, in which the protagonist enters a 'parallel world' were a great inspiration to C S Lewis who regarded MacDonald as his 'Master'. His friends included Lewis Carroll, John Ruskin and Frederick Denison Maurice. He admired the work of William Blake and was a friend of Dr James John Garth Wilkinson, the homeopathic physician and translator of Swedenborg. In later years MacDonald, who suffered from lung haemorrhages, wintered in Bordighera on the Italian Riviera in a villa bought for him by wealthy admirers. He died in Surrey in September 1905.

Oscar Milosz was born in 1877, in Cereja, a region formerly tied to Lithuania but at that time annexed to Russia. When he was twelve, the family moved to France, and French would be the language in which he wrote throughout his life. In 1899, at the age of 22, he published *Le Poème des Décadences,* and the theme of decline runs throughout his work. Between 1902 and 1910, he travelled Europe, reading extensively, particularly the work of Kant, Schopenhauer and Plato. Swedenborg's thoughts on conjugial love are echoed in *L'Amoureuse Initiation* (1910), a novel in which the protagonist renounces sex for a greater love, the love of God. On December 14, 1914 came *'la nuit d'illumination'* (the night of illumination), in which he glimpsed *'le soleil spirituel'* (the spiritual sun). Proud of his aristocratic roots, he was keen to promote the interests of Lithuania: in 1920, after France recognized the country's independence, he became its Chargé d'Affaires. Over the next two decades, he published collections of Lithuanian songs and stories. He also wrote the poems which won him his reputation as a mystic: *Ars Magna* (1924) and *Les Arcanes* (1927). Combining spiritual insights with references to science, philosophy, religion and art, these are poems in which he reclaims the Ancient Greek concept of *sophia*: knowledge combined with wisdom. Towards the end of his life, he met his young nephew, Czeslaw Milosz, and the Polish poet subsequently acknowledged his influence. Oscar died in 1939 of cancer, shortly before the breakout of World War II, in which he predicted the loss of Lithuania's independence.

Coventry Patmore was born in Essex in 1823 and was educated at home by his father, a reasonably well-known novelist and drama critic. In 1846 he became an assistant librarian at the British Museum and worked there for nearly twenty years. In 1847 he married Emily Augusta Andrews. Already a published poet, he was much admired by the Pre-Raphaelite Brotherhood and contributed to their journal, *The Germ*. Millais used his early poem, 'The Woodman's Daughter' (1844) as the subject for one of his paintings. He is most famous for *The Angel in the House*, a long narrative poem (Part I 1854 and Part II 1856) in praise of married love, inspired by Emily and his devotion to her. Patmore was also influenced by Swedenborg's *Conjugial Love* and the importance of the chastity of marriage. Emily died in 1862 and *The Angel in the House* was followed by a sequel, *The Victories of Love*, in 1863. In 1864 he was received into the Roman Catholic Church and in the following year he married Marianne Byles, another Catholic convert. Marianne's wealth enabled him to give up his job at the British Museum and buy a large estate in Sussex. His later volume of poems, *The Unknown Eros* (1878), is remarkable for its intense Catholic spirituality and erotic mysticism. He also published several books of prose including *Principle in Art* (1879), *Religio Poetae* (1893) and *The Rod, the Root and the Flower* (1895). After Marianne's death he married Harriet Robson, his children's governess. In his later years he formed friendships with Gerard Manley Hopkins, Alice Meynell and Francis Thompson. *The Angel in the House* was reprinted in a cheap edition in 1887. It was estimated that a million copies had been sold by the time of his death but the poem became associated with a particular view of Victorian womanhood and fell from favour. The fatal blow was perhaps delivered by Virginia Woolf when she wrote, in *A Room of One's Own* (1929), of the necessity of killing 'the Angel in the House'. Patmore died at Lymington, Hampshire in 1896.

Edgar Allan Poe was born January 19, 1809 in Boston, Massachusetts, USA. He was orphaned at 2 years old and fostered by a Virginia merchant, John Allan, whose name he took, though he was never legally adopted. He lived in England from 1815-20. In his turbulent youth he briefly attended the University of Virginia, joined the US Army under an assumed name, and was dismissed from West Point. He was employed as an editor for various magazines while he wrote some of his best-known work including his only commercial success *The Conchologist's First Book* (1839). Poe's first collection of short stories, *Tales of the Grotesque and Arabesque*, was published in 1840 featuring 'The Fall of the House of Usher', which spoke of studying Swedenborg's *Heaven and Hell*. After an earlier romantic disappointment, Poe married his 13-year-old cousin, Virginia, in 1836 who died of tuberculosis eleven years later and to whom he dedicated 'Annabel Lee' (1849). Poe was an influential literary critic although his poem 'The Raven' (1845) is acknowledged to be his most famous work. His short story, 'The Murders of the Rue Morgue' (1841) is considered the first modern detective story. Poe's atmospheric style and potent psychological subject matter has inspired entire genres of fiction and the work of many authors, filmmakers and musicians show his influence including Jorge Luis Borges, Jules Verne, Proust, Dostoevsky, and Nabokov. Poe suffered from depression and in 1848 he attempted suicide. He died October 7, 1849 in Baltimore, Maryland under mysterious circumstances.

| Index |